Boogie

Boogie

Life on a Merry-Go-Round

Michael Olesker

Apprentice
House Press
Loyola University Maryland

First Edition

Casebound ISBN: 978-1-62720-369-2
Paperback ISBN: 978-1-62720-370-8
Ebook ISBN: 978-1-62720-371-5

Printed in the United States of America

Design by Camryn Simmerman
Author photo by Jim Burger

Published by Apprentice House Press

Apprentice House Press
Loyola University Maryland
4501 N. Charles Street
Baltimore, MD 21210
410.617.5265
www.ApprenticeHouse.com
info@ApprenticeHouse.com

Dedicated to Isabelle and Sam Alter
For that not-so-distant time when
They're old enough
To read.

Contents

Chapter One

"You Either Liked Me, or Hated Me, or You Were Afraid of Me"

In his chaotic youth on the streets of mid-century Baltimore, Leonard (Boogie) Weinglass confronted all financial difficulties with a series of hustles, some legal, ranging from two-cent deposits on swiped soda bottles to football pools to the blank report cards he sold to classmates looking to sneak a fast one past unsuspecting parents.

Such activities, across a lifetime, will fall somewhere between a misdemeanor and a smile.

You want examples, you start with the March, 1982, night of the grand premiere of Barry Levinson's movie, "Diner," at the Senator Theater. The Senator was located on York Road, where the gentiles lived. Organizers of the premiere chose the Senator since all the movie theaters of Jewish northwest Baltimore were reduced to memory by 1982.

The Ambassador was gone, and so was the Forest. Also lost were the Uptown, the Gwynn and the Avalon. And, never to be forgotten, the Crest, where the teenage Boogie plotted the encounter between an open box of popcorn which rested in the center of his lap, and his unsuspecting date's hand.

That particular moment's captured in "Diner," with the actor Mickey Rourke playing Boogie, but it happened in real life more than 20 years earlier. You can ask any of those guys who mistakenly bet money that Boogie couldn't pull it off. Women are naturally appalled by this incident, and many men claim to be when in the presence of these women. But the guys who lost the bet are all here tonight for the movie premiere, and they're still talking about the popcorn story as though it happened yesterday.

So much of it remains fresh in people's minds who have known this Boogie Weinglass character somewhere over the past eight decades. To some, he's rascally and charming and immeasurably generous; to others, he's locked eternally into adolescence. To those who know him for the past 20 minutes or the length of a lifetime, he is unforgettable.

"If you knew Boogie back in the day," he says, lapsing into the comic third-person he occasionally uses to refer to himself, "you either liked me, or hated me, or you were afraid of me."

In Baltimore, where he grew up in the post-World War II years, he writes a history that becomes municipal legend. He breaks all North American scholastic records for most suspensions in a single semester, and threatens mayhem in order to graduate high school, at which time he was 20 years old. He's arguably the city's finest white varsity basketball player on those occasions when he's academically eligible. He makes his mark on a local TV dance program, where his jitterbugging helps bestow a life-long nickname. This boy can boogie. He woos, and wins, a succession of young ladies undeterred by what

Boogie self-effacingly calls his "big nose," his skinny frame and unimposing height, and his empty pockets.

Then he grows up, sort of.

Approaching the fullness of eight decades, he's lived mostly in Aspen since the second of his three marriages. He built a ranch eventually valued at roughly $50 million. He's in the city's Hall of Fame. People there talk about the "boogiefication" of the town. Not everyone means this as compliment. He made many millions from his Merry-Go- Round clothing chain and his string of Boogie's Diners. When national magazines wrote profiles about him, Boogie nakedly confessed to everything, including the prodigious gambling and the recovery. Also, the legions of women. He is unwrapped at all times.

Among those who are multi-millionaires, he may be the country's easiest touch. His financial advisers say he's given away tens of millions—just in the past decade—and millions more before that. He gives to strangers who need medical help, or assistance with the rent, or a shot in the arm. He's given to entire armies of troubled kids. He gives to people he meets in a deli line. His financial advisor, Josh Scheinker, says, "He wants to make as much money as he can because he wants to give away as much as he can. It's every single charity from Baltimore to Aspen, it's individuals in trouble who he's never met, it's ex-wives, it's ex-girlfriends, it's guys in Baltimore who go back to the '50s with him who are having a little trouble."

The generosity, says an old friend, comes from "a genuinely good heart, a hunger to ensure people's love, and a wish to buy brownie points to get into heaven."

The big money came from Merry-Go-Round, the company he created and then expanded like crazy. It started with rebellious bell bottom pants and strategically torn jeans and goldfish swimming in platform shoes, and it went to nearly fifteen hundred stores across the country, nearly fifteen thousand employees, and a billion dollars in annual sales. Forbes Magazine called it Number 34 on its list of the 200 best corporations in America. Then, when Boogie let others take over the business, the whole Merry-Go- Round thing went away.

The premiere night of "Diner" brings back the start of this breathless lifetime ride. At the Senator Theater, March of 1982, everybody's still getting seated while Boogie's off in a corner catching up with director Barry Levinson. I'm there, too. At this time, I'm writing a column for the Baltimore Sun newspaper, which has given me previous entrée into the lives of each of these men.

Weinglass and Levinson know each other since their nights at the Hilltop Diner. Each is a lesson in avoiding premature judgment based on high school transcript. You never know how people will turn out. Levinson graduated last in his class at Forest Park High School and didn't know he'd made it until the final day of school. He becomes Hollywood royalty. Weinglass, who attended several different high schools, but only on occasion, is practically eligible for Medicare by the time he gets his diploma.

In fact, there was a conversation he and I had, some years earlier, in which we took note of each other's age.

"How come," he asked, "I'm four years older than you, but I was only two years ahead of you in school?"

"Because," I said, "you went through high school on the five-year plan."

"Yeah," he said. "I'd take tests, and write all the answers on my arms to cheat. But I'd write all the wrong answers."

But there's a more telling piece of that conversation that stays with me, which I wrote down and later put into a newspaper column. Boogie's talking about his first taste of big money, when Merry-Go-Round was taking off and he and a fellow named Harold Goldsmith were expanding beyond their most fertile imaginings.

Boogie decides to join a Baltimore country club. He's moved Merry-Go-Round's corporate headquarters from Atlanta to Baltimore by this time, and a country club's a good place to play a little tennis, show off a person's money and, who knows, maybe have a few laughs. Or not.

"There were all these rich people there," he said, "and not one of them knew how to enjoy their money. Their lives were wrapped around making more money, instead of enjoying it. And I told myself, 'That's never gonna be me.'"

Enjoyment, he's clearly had, and sometimes paid a heavy price.

But now, on the night of "Diner's" premiere, he and Levinson are talking about another, earlier time, before there was any money or fame for either of them. Though they both went to Forest Park High School, Boogie only stayed for half the ride. The cops marched him off in handcuffs. Across adolescence and slightly beyond, he would attend three different high schools, not including a few more for summer school each year.

Three decades later, Anne Bennett Swingle will write, in Baltimore Magazine, "There are maybe fifty thousand people in Baltimore today who claim to have gone to school with Boogie—and they may all be right."

I first saw him when we both went to high school at Baltimore City College. Between classes one day in the fall of 1960, I'm walking along a first-floor hallway when a classmate, with a little awe in his voice, says, "See that guy? That's Boogie Weinglass."

I'd only been at City for a few months but I knew the name, because everybody in school knew it.

"He's important," my classmate said solemnly.

"Why?" I said. "Because he's on the basketball team?"

"No. Because he's the guy to go to if you need a blank report card."

Boogie had a few hundred of them. There were rumors he'd broken in to Baltimore public school headquarters, down on 25ᵗʰ Street, but nobody knew for sure. It was all part of the legend. The important thing was, he had them, and he was selling them.

His days were for attending school, but only when necessary, and nights were for hanging out.

In that crowded little era, the guys like Boogie could sit all night long in some little booth at the Hilltop Diner. They'd talk about the town's great love affair with the Baltimore Colts football team, whose snatching 25 years later would leave fans utterly bereft, and leave Baltimore wandering in the football wasteland for years.

And who leads the attempt to bring a professional football team back to Baltimore, but the grown-up Boogie. Now he's a multi-millionaire, ready to spend big. Sixty thousand fans will gather at Memorial Stadium, where they chant, "Give Boogie the ball" over and over, like a municipal hallelujah chorus. You can hear their cries from 33ʳᵈ Street, where the Colts played, all the way to Reisterstown Road where the famous diner used to be.

Directly across the street from the diner was the Hilltop Shopping Center and the Crest Theater, where Boogie pulled off his popcorn bet—the perfect place to premiere "Diner."

But the Crest's gone by 1982, along with all those other northwest Baltimore theaters supported mainly by the Jews.

The Crest, once a showplace, became a branch of the dreary Motor Vehicle Administration. The Forest became the Nation of Islam's Muhammad Mosque Number Six, and the Uptown became the Lord's Church of Baltimore.

The Jews fled their post-war homes, just like millions of white gentiles in countless American cities, and many old neighborhood theaters emptied and died. This is why they're opening "Diner" over at the Senator, where Jews back in Barry Levinson's post-war era rarely ventured. They knew their place.

Back then, Baltimore was an ethnic mosaic. There was Little Italy down in southeast Baltimore, and further east, there were Poles and Germans and Greeks, separated by casual slander of the era. Sometimes they lived directly across the street from each other. But the streets could seem wide as the Atlantic to anyone wishing to venture across.

People kept their distance. There were Catholic school nuns who warned their students not to mix with public school kids. "You never know," the children were informed, "which ones might be Protestants."

There were teenage dances. Here were Italian teens. Over on the other side, Irish. One night at a place called Keith's Rooftop, some Italian boy crossed the floor and attempted to dance with an Irish girl. Mayhem ensued.

The fighting stopped only when the band struck up The Star Spangled Banner and everybody in the place instinctively stood at attention. Patriots, every one.

Don't even think about racial mixing. In post-war Baltimore, the exodus to suburbia begins at the first hint of black people moving in to white neighborhoods. This happens with a frenzy where Boogie Weinglass lived with his parents and two older brothers.

There was Irving, known as Eggy for the shape of his head, and Jackie, known for his ball playing. The family rented a row house with a little front porch on west Baltimore's Baker Street, a few blocks off of Fulton Avenue, which was the west-side historic dividing line between the city's blacks and whites.

As post-war blacks began crossing Fulton Avenue, whites moved out. All except the Weinglass family and those other whites lacking money to join the exodus. There was money coming in, but more going out. The family had a little corner grocery store, but whatever profit it brought, Solomon Weinglass, Boogie's father, gambled away.

And so there was much anguish. The mother, the former Nettie Snessell, was a Polish refugee still grappling with English, and with memory of atrocity. The father, Solomon, got out of Germany just before the fullness of Hitler's genocide. In America, their sons learned the rudiments of scuffling.

When the family finally makes the move up to northwest Baltimore, to Violet Avenue off of lower Reisterstown Road, they were late entries into this first sweeping American exodus.

For about a decade, though, we have Nettie and her three boys on Violet Avenue. The boys' lives consist of street ball and pool halls and hustling for spare change. Nettie's activity consists of chasing after them. The father, Solomon, leaves early, first to a sanitarium with tuberculosis and then from marital separation when Nettie's had enough with the gambling. And then Solomon dies young.

This leaves Boogie running the streets and finding hangouts such as the Hilltop Diner and Benny's pool room.

Benny's, that's where Boogie matriculates whenever he's cutting school or can't find a pickup basketball game. If he's not shooting pool there, he's playing ping pong, in which he boasts he can beat anybody not Asian. If he's not playing ping pong, he's hustling football pools, the little gambling cards with point spreads which are his primary source of income. This, while in high school.

Also, Benny's is where he bumps into the young Harold Goldsmith. Boogie's never laid eyes on Harold, but Harold knows about Boogie because—well, who doesn't?

The legends are already taking hold, especially one that's endearing to Goldsmith: Boogie can fight.

"Boogie, would you help me?" Goldsmith implores one day at Benny's. "We had a bet, and this guy won't pay me."

This is where it begins. One guy does another a small favor. A fist fight ensues. And the fight will change everything in two people's lives. Never mind hustling football pools for Boogie, and never mind Harold collecting rents on his father's slum properties forever. Those days will soon be over.

Within a few years, Boogie will create a clothing store called Merry-Go-Round, and Harold, seeing the beginnings of a good thing, will sign on a little later, when the company's already growing. Then the two of them will create a billion-dollar empire that reaches across the entire country. They remove the grey flannel suits of the era and replace them with bell bottoms and torn tee shirts and tattered jeans and platform shoes.

Yesterday's shmattes become a generation's street fashions.

America wants to be young again, and Boogie will spend a lifetime outracing time itself.

This takes us back to the night of the "Diner" movie premiere. Much of the old gang from the Hilltop Diner's there. There's Levinson, of course, at the start of his remarkable directing career. Some arrive wearing dress-up movie premiere outfits. Boogie's wearing jeans and a tee shirt and cowboy boots, and his hair's in a pony tail. But his ride's pretty cool. He's in his chauffeur-driven Rolls Royce.

As it happens, I'm seated directly behind him as the movie plays. Everybody's watching the scene where Boogie and Fenwick spot a pretty girl riding a horse as they drive somewhere along Greenspring Valley Road, out there in the wealthy Baltimore County horse breeding area.

In the darkness of the Senator Theater, the real Boogie turns around and chuckles my way.

"That can't be me," he says. "I was never north of Belvedere Avenue in my life."

It's his little joke. Belvedere Avenue, that's the hallowed old grounds of Benny's pool room. By this time, though, Leonard (Boogie) Weinglass had made it long past Belvedere Avenue, long past Benny's and the Hilltop Diner, and long past anyone's most fabulous fantasies.

Chapter Two

The Beginning of Hunger

At the height of his obsessions, Boogie Weinglass was betting heavily on baseball games every summer night. Each autumn, there was football gambling. And in all seasons, when he went to Las Vegas, he would take over entire high-roller card tables.

And yet, for a little perspective: the odds on his rise from sheer poverty to so much wealth are longer than the most lunatic bet he ever placed.

He enters the world October 21, 1941, the last of three boys born to Nettie and Solomon Weinglass. The date is not quite seven weeks before the attack on Pearl Harbor and the entrance of the United States into World War II. Nettie and Solomon are immigrants fortunate to be among the living even before America plunges into the bloodshed.

Each escapes Europe in the 1930s, inches before Hitler's murderers can get to them. Solomon made it out of Germany, but most of his family did not. Nettie escaped Poland but her parents and siblings did not. The war swallowed them up. In all the accounts Boogie heard through the years, Nettie stowed away on a ship to America. She hid inside a large carton with holes punched in it so she could breathe. She remained inside the box for much of the voyage. That was the easy part of it. In Poland, she witnessed some barbarian military officer slash open her twin sister's throat.

That moment haunts her forever. As she lights Shabbat candles every Friday evening, Nettie sobs inconsolably for the sister. Her young sons watch. The mother's grief stays with them, and becomes an emotional touchstone Leonard will talk about for the rest of his life.

Here, he says, is the genesis of some of his street fighting. Some bigot makes a remark about the Jews, he'll pay for it. Boogie recalls hearing a lot of this mindless anti-Jew slander through his school years. He carries a natural sweetness, and a hunger to please, but a snap temper that develops early and stays.

"Hitler," he says.

Ask about his temper, and the countless fights, and this is the reflexive answer. It stays with him. He says this as though Hitler himself had drawn the knife across the poor woman's throat and caused his mother's ritual tears all those Friday nights.

"We had an Orthodox Jewish home," he recalls. "My mother kept kosher. Separate dishes, meat and dairy. Every Friday evening, we had no lights on in the house, only candles until Saturday sundown. My mother would cry as she lit them. She remembered the knife across her sister's throat. And my mother and her mother watched it happen."

The post-war generation came of age with intimate emotional ties to the genocide. But, for years, silence dominated. The wounds were still too raw, and the crime too fresh, to put into words. The term "holocaust" didn't enter the jargon for more than a decade after the war ended. Even the Hebrew schools worked around it.

"Neither of my parents talked about it much," Weinglass remembered. "My father had one brother that survived, an Uncle Max, who we met one time on a trip up to New York. He was a big man with white hair, and he had the camp number tattooed on his arm. The other brothers never made it out.

"My mother lost her whole family. But, somehow, she got on this ship, and she got into one of these cartons big enough to hold a refrigerator. They were afraid there might be soldiers who'd inspect the ship. So she stayed in the box for a few days. She told me she had to pee in her pants in there. She told me that story once, and I never wanted to hear it again."

Nettie and Solomon met and married after their arrival in Baltimore, an introduction arranged by the local Associated Jewish Charities, which assisted those fortunate enough to get out of Europe. They were each about forty. A romance for the ages, it was not. The sound that stays with their youngest son is incessant hollering, always in Yiddish.

The Weinglass boys will be raised where Yiddish is the primary language in the home. Then they'll attend a parochial school, the Talmudical Academy, where Hebrew is the primary language. By the time Leonard reaches public school in the seventh grade, English is considered a second language, or third. His late development with it will shroud his classroom years.

The parents are safely out of Europe, but they adjust haltingly to life in the new world. Solomon is slightly more Americanized than his wife. Within the bounds of poverty, he dresses nicely and wears a fedora tilted at a stylish angle. Nettie lights the Shabbat candles with a babushka covering her head.

"For me, the Jewish thing was tied in tight with the holocaust," Weinglass says. "My mother crying all the time. Both of their families wiped out. It made me very hardened about any kind of prejudiced people. Any kind. And I remember my dad telling me one time, when I was little and some guy punched me, Don't take any shit off anybody."

The words are expressed inelegantly, but they stay with him. His parents were defenseless victims, but weakness will never befall the rambunctious sons. Their father is a cadaverous little man slowly dying in front of everyone, but Leonard, soon to be known as Boogie, will spend a lifetime out-running everything, sickness and poverty and age itself.

The family lives at 2207 Baker Street, in west Baltimore, a crowded white working class neighborhood of modest row houses with little front porches. You go to Baker Street today, and your eyeballs begin to bleed.

There are neighborhood churches with all windows and doors boarded up, and the faithful long gone, as though God himself has abandoned them. On each block of Baker Street, homes are falling apart. Vagrant wads of trash blow about. On the Weinglass's old block, there's a string of empty, rotting homes on both sides of the street.

The neighborhood was never exactly Versailles, but its true decay commenced with the end of the war and the abandonment of huge swaths of the city of Baltimore.

Nettie and Solomon ran a corner grocery store two blocks from their home. This is the battleground of marital warfare. She runs the little place with her minimal English while watching over the two older boys, Jackie and Irving. Solomon plunders the cash register every day and goes off to feed an addiction with Boogie in tow.

"Take Label," Nettie cries out.

"Label," that's Hebrew for Leonard. "Boogie patrol," his youngest son will one day refer to his father's daily supervision.

With the grocery store, there's always steady money coming in but more going out. Solomon gambles everything away.

He gambles at poker and gin, and he gambles with his life. He sits in a little room at some crummy little Democratic political clubhouse each day, where the air is filled with cigarette smoke. Everybody in the room puffs away. Solomon goes through three packs of unfiltered Camels each day. Three or four tables in the room, everybody smoking, and a restless young Label waiting around for hours in this atmosphere.

Sometimes Solomon gives him a nickel or a dime to buy an ice cream cone or a candy bar. But these do nothing for the smoke. Label stands on the edges of the card games and years later remembers rubbing his eyes the whole time he's there.

"Today, you walk into a room, there's an intake and an out-take," he says. "But this is nothing but a room. No ventilation at all. And every one of these guys are smoking cigarettes, and they're all breathing in the smoke. And my father's losing whatever money my mother's taking in every day back at the store."

This leads to unrelenting poverty, including hunger. He remembers his mother hiding food for him so the older brothers can't scarf it all down before Label gets home from running the streets. The brothers are older, so they've started playing ball. The game's over, they head home, and they're famished. Label's still out there, hustling for a few cents wherever he can find them.

"I'd go up to Easterwood Park and look for soda bottles," he says. "Get two cents deposit on the regular bottles and a nickel on the big ones. People would buy a soda at the store and take it to the park and then toss it away. I'd scavenge. I'd compete with the other poor kids. I wasn't the only one doing it. We'd all see a bottle and run for it at the same time and fight for it.

"What I didn't find at the park, I'd walk up and down the alleys and look for bottles. People would put their empties on the back porch until they went to the store again. I'd grab 'em off the porches. And I'd go through the trash cans in the alley, and look for bottles that people threw out. I'd make enough to get some bread or milk for my mother."

As Melinda Greenberg will write, years later in Baltimore's Jewish Times, he was already learning "what it was to want."

At home, Nettie wastes nothing. If she finishes with a jar of peanut butter, the jar gets scraped clean, then washed, and becomes a drinking glass. Apples are eaten to the core and beyond. No vegetable ever goes wasted. All clothing is ultimately worn by all three sons.

Other families put coverings over floors to protect against children tracking mud into the house. They put plastic covers over couches and chairs to protect them from the hyperactive young. Nettie hasn't got money for rugs or seat covers, so she improvises. She spreads newspapers over everything, imagining these will protect furniture and floors. Instead, the newspapers lie there, and they get newsprint over everything, so that the house seems dingier and more disheveled than ever. Her youngest son still recalls the dread that any friend might enter the house and see the newspapers spread everywhere.

The boys spend as much time outside the house as possible. When Label's not scrounging for soda bottle deposits—and then handing over the money to his mother, maybe a dollar on a really good day—he's out in the alley, racing across rooftops.

"That was our entertainment," he says. "We'd go out in the alley behind the houses. There were garages back there. You'd have maybe five in a row, and then there's a space between them, and then more garages. Me and my friends would climb up on the roofs. We'd get a running start, and then you have to time it perfect for the separation, which is about five feet apart.

"That's a pretty good drop to the ground, especially for a kid. You have to plant your foot and kick off good to get to the other garage. We had one kid who fell and broke his jaw. He hit it on the other garage, going down. But I was lucky, I was pretty athletic, even then."

His childhood was a time of the coal man and the ice man making home deliveries. So did the Koester's bread man and the Cloverland milk man. Then there were street A-rabs, black men riding their rickety old horse-drawn wagons and splitting the air with their cries, announcing fresh fruits and vegetables. Nettie's a regular customer.

For a long time, those street A-rabs were the only blacks on the west side of Fulton Avenue, which was that unofficial racial dividing line in west Baltimore. Blacks on one side, whites on the other, and Fulton Avenue is the DMZ. It was that way for generations. Now, in World War II's aftermath, came a time of domestic convulsion.

As the young whites come home from the fighting, they're hungry to get on with their lives. Many want nothing to do with living near the colored. They've never actually met these black people, but they've absorbed the ritual slander they've heard all their lives.

In places like west Baltimore's Baker Street, where the Weinglass family lives, whites are moving off to suburban tracts that once seemed distant as Paris. As more whites leave, more blacks move in.

This is stunning business to a city with a segregated history. In Baltimore at this time, the largest drug store chain, Read's, refuses to allow any people of color to sit at lunch counters. It stays this way until the mid 1950s. It's 1956 before the city removes "White" and "Colored" signs from all of its public buildings. The state teachers association remains segregated into the 1950s, and so does the city bar association. Into the 1950s, there are no black firemen or bus drivers or cabbies.

Across much of the country, including Baltimore, the public schools will be segregated until 1954, when the U.S. Supreme Court demands integration.

For generations, the city of Baltimore went to great legal effort to keep black people in their place—away from whites. First, with an early-century ruling that prevented blacks from moving to white residential areas. Then, with private gentleman's agreements to bar blacks - and Jews - from moving into certain areas.

But now, with the ending of the war, whites start evacuating blocks at a time. In March of 1945, there were about 50 black families all along the old line of racial separation, broad, lengthy Fulton Avenue. Four months later, hundreds of empty homes were available to them.

All of this was intensified by real estate agents looking to cash in on everyone's anxieties. They made phone calls, sent letters, slipped circulars under front doors. The message was always the same: the neighborhood is changing, so don't be the last to get out. The Weinglass parents knew all of this, and their children intuited something about it, too. It was the dread sense of being left behind.

For Nettie and Solomon, though, it evoked recent memories: of wartime Europe, and of people all around them trying to escape while there was still time, and of ethnic differences dividing people who knew little of each other.

As their West Baltimore neighborhood changes, the money situation worsens. Solomon gambles everything away, including his life. The smoke works its way into him. While they're still on Baker Street, he suffers the first miserable symptoms of the tuberculosis which will lead to the end of the Weinglass marriage, and the end of Solomon.

They're not the only struggling family in the neighborhood. Whites remaining around Baker Street have little money—it's why they stay - and the incoming blacks have even less. Race has dictated this. Now the streets are getting tougher. There's talk of increased crime. You see police more often now.

And Solomon's still over at the clubhouse, as long as there's a card game to be played. One winter evening, Nettie's put dinner on the table, and there's a pounding on the back door leading to the alley.

"Somebody's pounding with fists," Weinglass remembers. "Like they're gonna break it down."

Nettie goes to the back door, and there in the evening chill stands her husband. He's totally unclothed. Some neighborhood tough guys have checked out his daily patterns. They know when he leaves the card game each evening, and they hit him when he happens to be carrying winnings.

"He got mugged by professionals, and he got beat up pretty bad," Weinglass says. "They take all your clothes, especially in shaky neighborhoods, because they know you might hide your money in your underwear, or your shoes and socks. So they just rip off everything, and run off, and later they look through it to see what they got.

"My father's standing there in the cold, and he's totally messed up, and my mother's hysterical. For her, it was like the Gestapo all over again, and her sister getting her throat cut. For me, it was my first real experience of understanding I was in a tough neighborhood. My father was no sissy. He was a sweet guy, but he was hardened, too. And they took everything."

Help from above is the only way out for the Weinglass family. The same Associated Jewish Charities that introduced Nettie and Solomon now comes through with enough money to move. They'll go where all the Jews are going now: to northwest

Baltimore, somewhere above a big commercial intersection called Park Circle with an amusement park there called Carlin's, which resembles the entrance to a dream.

They moved into a cramped row house with a narrow front yard at 2916 Violet Avenue, located several blocks above Park Circle. That landmark is important. It's the gateway to two of northwest Baltimore's great boulevards, Park Heights Avenue and Reisterstown Road. For those who landed somewhere above Park Circle in the post-war years, the feeling was relief. It signaled a sense of middle class status, or at least the ability to fake it.

The Weinglass family could never even fake it.

Solomon's heavy smoking was now catching up to him. Tuberculosis, which puts him in a sanitarium. Then marital separation, because Nettie can't take care of him, nor tolerate his gambling any longer.

"He's no good," Nettie tells the boys, always in Yiddish. "I work all day for the gelt, and he does nothing."

Solomon will live in a little rented room thereafter, several blocks from Violet Avenue. His sons will see him occasionally, but the separation is final.

"The whole thing," their youngest son reflects, "robbed me of my childhood."

Nettie sits at a Singer sewing machine on Violet Avenue. She does hemming and cuffing for neighbors so she can take in a few dollars. Winters, there's frost on the insides of the windows of the house because there's not enough money to pay for heat. Newspapers still cover the chairs and the floors. Nettie buys half a pound of baloney for the three boys to share. Neighbors don't have much themselves, but they know what it's like in the Weinglass home. Sometimes they drop by and leave a carton of milk for the boys to share.

And there's Label, holding on to some of his old instincts.

He's outside scrounging for discarded soda bottles so he can collect the two-cent deposits on them. Instead of the alleys around Baker Street, he's got the alleys around Violet Avenue. Instead of Easterwood Park, he's now got the Towanda playground.

"Kids would have bottles of soda, and they'd toss it somewhere when they were done," he remembers. "So I'd grab it. A couple of cents meant a lot to me. I had a little mesh knapsack I'd carry around and stash the bottles. It'd hold four or five of the big bottles. Or I'd go up and down the alleys and swipe bottles off people's back porches before they could cash them in themselves. I'd go to all kinds of neighborhoods, just looking for bottles to grab."

At the end of a day's collecting, he'd stash the empties behind his own house and hope his mother didn't notice. But she did.

"She'd say, 'Label, what are you doing?' She sensed I was stealing off of people's porches, and it made her look sad. But I made a small living that way."

When he's not hustling soda bottles, he finds something else at the Towanda playground, where kids from the surrounding neighborhoods gather. He discovers he's a natural athlete. He's quick, he's scrappy and unafraid, and he can jump. Basketball or baseball, doesn't matter, the bigger kids want him in their games and on their teams.

He's got energy spilling out of him. He's challenging kids to races, and beats them. Sometimes they'll race for money, only a few cents, but it helps. Kid named Jan Abrams, who lived around the corner on Overview Avenue, remembers meeting him.

"I moved over from Druid Lake Drive," Abrams says, "and I'm standing with Skip Friedman, and I hear somebody say, 'I'll race you around the garages.' And it was Boogie. That was the start of a friendship."

Abrams sees what everybody sees: an undisciplined kid who has no guidance. A sweet kid, eager to please, but quick to pick a fight, too.

"One time," Abrams says, "we're playing cards in this guy's bedroom. Four of us up there. Boogie says, 'You owe me a quarter, I won.' Guy says, 'No, you didn't.' And, before you know it, they start fighting. Over a quarter. It's this little bedroom, and they're slugging it out. They're knocking things over, and I'm standing there with Bernie Rabinowitz, and we're laughing. So they stop fighting, and now they want to beat us up. Because we're laughing.

"I saw Boogie in a lot of fights over the years, and I never once saw him back down. Guys a lot bigger than him, too. He had the gumption and the heart."

Abrams remembers Solomon Weinglass living apart from the rest of the family. "Once in a while he'd see Boogie, who wasn't crazy about running into him. And the mother, Nettie, was like 80 years old. I mean, she was always old. She talked with an accent, and she dressed in shmattes. She was clearly from some other country. And she had no control. The only discipline he got was from his brother Jackie. He'd beat him up."

Nettie did her best, but she understood too little. Weinglass remembers playing ball at Towanda playground, and his mother would suddenly appear.

"She'd come down with a jar of milk," he says. "It was one of the old peanut butter jars. She didn't throw anything away.

She'd clean it out and use it. A jar of milk, and a banana and a sandwich.

"I was embarrassed. I'm trying to be a macho guy, and here comes my mother with milk in an old peanut butter jar. She meant well. But who wants his mother showing up where you're trying to be a tough guy?"

That was Nettie being sweet. Sometimes she'd demand her sons come home for lunch. When they balked, they paid for it. She'd break out a strap and chase them off the playing fields with all the other kids watching.

Solomon also shows up sometimes, on rare days when he feels strong enough to get outside. It's not often. One time, when Label's maybe 12 years old, some big kid at the playground punches him in the face.

"Might have been a Jewish thing, or just a bully," he remembers. "And I cried. By this time, my father was separated from my mother because he was sick and my mother couldn't take care of him. And she's still angry over the gambling, even though he's fighting for his life.

"So I go to my father and tell him what happened. He was very frail. He had a room on the second floor of a house on Keyworth Avenue, about five blocks from Violet Avenue. Second floor, and he can't even walk steps at this point. He was there for two years.

"And I start crying. He says, 'Label, why are you crying?' 'Big kid punched me.' He says, 'You go right up to him and punch him right in the nose. Which hand are you?' I showed him my right hand. He says, 'You punch in the nose with your right hand. And, when you do, follow with the other hand and keep punching.'

"He was adamant. I sat there for a while, and I stopped crying. He says, 'How big was he?' "A little bigger than me. Older, too.' 'Doesn't matter.' He sends me back to the playground. I see the guy. I'm a little nervous, but I'm motivated, right?

"He was talking to some other kid. I walked up to him and said, 'Hey.' And I smashed him in the mouth. I hit him good. Both his hands went to his mouth. Then I brought the left. He bent down and tried to get away. I gave him another right. And then, figuring he was bigger, I got out of there fast.

"I went back to my father, who was really proud. That was my first real fight, I guess. That's what made me a sicko. After that, anybody that tried to bully me, the fight starts."

Nettie holds on to her Orthodox Judaism. She walks to shule every Shabbat. She sends the boys to Talmudical Academy for schooling. In the public schools of America, children spend their days refining reading and writing skills in English, learning increasingly sophisticated mathematics, memorizing the history of the past few centuries.

At the Talmudical Academy, whose students casually refer to their school as T.A., there is little history taught that does not relate to 5,000 years ago. The public schools are drilling children on Washington and Lincoln and Christopher Columbus. At T.A., they spend their days studying Abraham, Isaac and Jacob. They do this in Hebrew. Late each afternoon, they study what the school refers to as a foreign language: English.

And so, while other American children take this language for granted, Boogie's got Yiddish at home and Hebrew at school. He's already falling behind in American language skills.

The school's vice principal was Rabbi Jacob A. Max. Later, when Boogie's donated lots of money each year to the school, the rabbi diplomatically describes him as "a child who ran from the classroom. We'd usually find him in the playground or in the woods behind the school."

He's no scholar, but he sticks around long enough for a bar mitzvah service at the Agudas Achim Synagogue. This is also his exit from Talmudical Academy, and from Hebrew in the classroom all day long, and his entrance into public school.

It doesn't take long to realize it's an awkward fit. At Garrison Junior High, and then at Pimlico Junior High, he finds that he's far behind academically. The hours spent at Hebrew left him deprived of English reading and writing skills. The years listening to Nettie and Solomon speaking Yiddish leave him far behind kids who have grown up unconsciously absorbing and refining their English skills.

And he looks at these public school kids, most of them from intact middle class homes, and knows in his bones that there are good things in their lives—new clothes, full lunches—that put his life to shame.

On Violet Avenue, the neighbors are learning about him, to an extent. They see a sweet kid who's in a tough spot. They see he's hustling for a few cents here and there. Once, he gets a 25-cent tip for running an errand. It felt, he says, like a $20 bill. Sometimes neighbors will give him money to go to the store and pick up a few things for them. Sometimes he forgets to come back.

He's ten years old and cutting grass in the summer and shoveling front walks when it snows. He's 13 when he gets his first legitimate job, making deliveries for a neighborhood pharmacy. The drug store gives him a bike to make the deliveries.

He gets to know a lot of neighborhoods, and a lot of customers, including an older woman known to all as Kank, who is not precisely a mother figure.

Chapter Three

Benny's Poolroom

On this blustery day in January, 1958, the 16-year old Boogie Weinglass stands at the corner of Reisterstown Road and Violet Avenue with his thumb in the air and larceny in his heart. He's faced with a choice. He can stand there hoping to hitch a ride, with the winter wind cutting into him like a blade, or he can swipe somebody's car for a little while.

You want a snapshot of this kid's early years, here it is: he's out there, alone in the cold, while many are living in comfort and warmth. This is what he perceives all around him. So he has a choice: anger that he's been locked out of the game, or spontaneous, seat-of-the-pants creation of his own rules of living.

Or both.

By now, each is within his repertoire. Here and there, he's been swiping cars ever since he was old enough to learn the art of the hot-wire. Go on, call a cop. But he's not completely without conscience in such matters. On several occasions, he'll drive some pilfered car wherever he needs to go, and carefully park it, and then put in a call to the Northwest District Police, whose number he knows by heart.

"There's a stolen '56 Chevy," he'll inform them, "parked on Belvedere Avenue, right around the corner from the Harley's Carry-Out. The license plate is…"

"How do you know this?" some brilliant desk sergeant will ask.

At which point Boogie hangs up and goes about his business of the day. What's he supposed to do, stay on the phone? On most occasions, his daily business is found at Benny's Poolroom, Reisterstown Road and Belvedere Avenue, where Boogie matriculates when he ought to be somewhere else, such as 10th grade.

"That's where I got my real education," he says.

From his mother's house on Violet Avenue, Benny's is a straight shot up Reisterstown Road, a little too far to walk but a short drive. It's also the place where many remarkable things commence in Boogie's life. He plays a decent game of pool here, and might win a couple of bucks. He plays a great game of ping pong, where he can hustle even more dough. He has a few of his most memorable fist fights in the place, one of which involves the defense of Harold Goldsmith, with whom he will one day amass what feels like all of the money in the entire known world.

Benny's is run by a fellow named Benny Kit, short and bald, in short-sleeve shirts and dull khaki pants. Benny's pushing 60. He's got maybe a dozen pool tables in the place, widely spaced, a couple of ping pong tables, a little area for two card games, and three pinball machines which are in use until the place closes at one in the morning. Also, nice touch, a little food area with coddies and sodas and, on Saturdays, hot dogs cooked by Benny's wife Edith.

You reach the joint by walking up a flight of stairs. The place is pretty old, but it's clean. You see middle-aged losers and kids in their teens and twenties. They're all white, but it's an ethnic mix, mostly Jews and Italians and drapes. Some guys are funnier than others, but everybody's cutting up. And a lot of them have learned the art of the knock, and the use of sarcasm as verbal switchblade.

Guy misses an easy one.

"Nice shot, Minnesota Fats."

That sarcastic impulse—saying one thing while obviously meaning another—becomes a Jewish Baltimore verbal twitch and stays with a generation of people their entire lives.

It's there in "Diner," setting up the popcorn scene, when Mickey Rourke, as Boogie, announces, "I'm taking out Carol Heathrow."

"You're taking out Carol Heathrow?" says a stunned Fenwick, played by Kevin Bacon.

"No, *you're* taking her," says Boogie, as if such a miracle could possibly happen.

Or, in real-life northwest Baltimore of the era, some poor guy gets dressed up a little too sharp for a date.

"You're Hud," he's told, thus deflating all self-confidence.

It's shorthand. Hud is Gary Huddles, universally regarded as the best looking guy in northwest Baltimore, or anywhere in North America. "You're Hud" means the guy's fooling himself, he's trying too hard and made himself an easy target in the process.

This jargon becomes sink-or-swim impulse, a way to get your shot in before the other guy does. Sometimes it stings, sometimes it's a smile. It's also a way to develop a tough hide, or slink away in humiliation.

"Always the putdown, constant knocking," Barry Levinson remembers years later. "I don't know why, but it was always there. And I think a lot of it came from Jensky."

That's Ben Jensky, who's one of the crowd at Benny's and the Hilltop Diner. Jensky comes on like Don Rickles, before anybody's even heard of Rickles.

"Nice shoes," he'll tell somebody. "Where'd you get 'em, Read's?"

Read's is the local drug store chain. The way Huddles was regarded as the handsomest guy, Jensky was the funniest. Many who heard him tried talking like him. Maybe, Levinson says, "It started with him and spread to the wider group." It became a whole style of talking, a sensibility, and a way of confronting the whole world. You put the other guy down, it gives you a little elevation. It's comic defense mechanism. With every line, an ego dies.

Anybody owning up to some shortcoming unwittingly opens himself up to ridicule. Protect yourself, or face the consequences.

"Jensky was in one of the high school fraternities," Levinson says. "I don't remember which one. But all the fraternities had a big dance every year, and they'd name somebody Royalty. A fraternity boy and sorority girl, king and queen. And Jensky won, and it was his big claim to fame. Although some guys figured the vote was fixed."

But he won, which made him seem cool. You want to seem cool like Jensky, start talking like him. The jargon, and the attitude, took on a life of its own.

Sometimes, it stayed for a lifetime. Many years later, when Nettie Weinglass died, Boogie telephoned his friend Allan Charles to tell him the sad news.

"My mother died," he said.

Shocked at the news, Allan replied, "Your mother died?"

"No, *yours* did," said Boogie.

Anyway, for those who can't find an after-school pick-up ballgame around Reisterstown Road or Park Heights Avenue, Benny's Poolroom is the place to go, and this is the wise-guy jargon of the era: protect yourself, or pay the price.

Benny the proprietor's quite a fellow. He's such a guiding influence that, when he hears Boogie wants to gamble any of his money, Benny will place a fatherly arm around him and, for a percentage of the action, he will cover the bet.

There's a lot of gambling going on here. Upon reflection, Boogie believes this is where he started his serious wagering. He bets on the house games, but graduates from this. He'll bet on anything. He'll bet on ballgames, which he studies, or on thoroughbred horse racing or European soccer, about which he knows nothing at all. He'll bet on foot races, often up Reisterstown Road and occasionally naked, in which Boogie is himself a participant. Gambling is his DNA legacy from Solomon, which his brothers have also inherited.

By his mid-teens, Boogie's becoming a street legend around northwest Baltimore. Putting his Talmudical Academy days behind him, he's enrolled at Garrison Junior High School, where no one confuses him with college material. Or high school material, for that matter.

He's not bad with spoken English, but he's years behind with the written word, whatever the subject. School isn't just a chore, it's a daily embarrassment, as are his hand-me-down clothes. He admits none of this to anyone, since any sign of weakness is fodder for the putdown. Everybody's trying to talk like Jensky. What do you do, admit you're flunking three subjects? Of course not. Instead, you find a way to change the subject. Instead of risking vulnerability, you act out.

The guys at the pool hall and the diner understand this, and they also know he's got a snap temper. So nobody messes with him. Even Jensky knows to lay off.

"Fighting, always fighting," Boogie reflects many years later. "Getting in trouble with teachers. Talking in class, showing off. A lot of my fights started because I didn't have the right clothes. I wasn't angry, so much as envious. Plus, I'd hear somebody make a remark about Jews. Not necessarily aimed at me, but I was in earshot. 'Those fuckin' Jews,' you know? I didn't let it pass. 'Which one of you said that?'

"Lot of guys would turn away. They're afraid, or they didn't want to get involved, they didn't want to get in trouble. I had a lot of Jewish friends who didn't get in fights. They didn't want to hear it. But maybe their parents' relatives weren't killed by Hitler."

The Nazis are a recurring theme when he talks about fighting—but it's only a start.

This was the post-war era when many northwest Baltimore fathers were starting to carve out successful careers, and mothers stayed at home coddling children who grew up with certain benefits taken for granted: the latest in stylish clothing, and cars to drive when they turned 16, which they showed off at school every day. And then summers, where those who didn't go to camp lazed around the country club swimming pool.

Boogie had none of this, and resented those who had it and flaunted it.

"I had guys call me a dirtball because of the way I dressed," he says. "Fraternity boys who lived around upper Park Heights. They're wearing button-down shirts and Ivy League stuff, and I'm wearing my brothers' hand-me-downs. Rich guys. Or, they seemed rich to me. I had my brother's khakis on, and my mother had to tie the waist together with a safety pin. One of those guys would say something about it."

There were house parties he'd hear about, but he wasn't invited. There were Greek letter fraternities, but he lacked the right clothes. There were private dances, which he'd crash. Let somebody tell him he didn't belong, and they'd pay for it.

The class consciousness—the great divide between Boogie and the kids with any money—was highlighted one time when he asked a girl for a date. They were classmates at Forest Park High School. The girl had some money, but Boogie had some self-confidence by this time. At Forest Park, he was a star on the basketball team.

"What time can I pick you up?" he remembers asking.

"How about eight o'clock?" She's smiling, and he's feeling pretty good.

"What's your address?" he asks. "I'll need it for the cab."

The girl appears confused.

"What do you mean, 'cab?'" As if she's never in her whole life heard the term.

"I don't have a car," he says.

"You're not driving?" she says.

Like there's something wrong with him, Boogie remembers decades later. There's still resentment in his voice after all this time. She's not just saying no to a date, she's defining his outcast social status.

"I'm not going out with you," she says.

"Not even tactfully," he says, looking back. "You know how I felt? I felt really, really poor."

It feeds into the class distinctions. He'll look elsewhere. Weekends you can find him at dances, maybe at a rec center or a synagogue social hall, which are open to all. And he loves to dance, which makes him something of a catch among teenage boys.

You go to dances of that era, and you'll see girls jitterbugging with other girls. There's nothing sexual about it, they're just eager to get out on the floor. There's a slight shortage of guys. They're over in some corner of the room, by the potato chips. If it's summer, they're talking about how many hits Brooks Robinson got last night. If it's fall, they're talking about Unitas and the Colts. Some of them consider dancing a little less than manly.

But Boogie loves to dance, and he's good at it. This gives him entrée to lots of girls who otherwise wouldn't give him a look. And it alerts somebody who has a connection to TV's Buddy Deane teenage dance program, which is such a pop culture force in Baltimore that, four decades later, it becomes the subject of a John Waters Broadway phenomenon called "Hairspray."

Much of teenage America watches the Dick Clark TV dance program every afternoon, but not Baltimore. Here, the Buddy Deane Show is so popular, it's shown live from TV Hill for a couple of hours five afternoons a week. It runs from 1957 to 1964, when its racial segregation finally becomes an embarrassment. The kids who are regulars on the show tell Deane they'd be fine if blacks are invited in—but their parents would never let it happen, they say. So the show remains a ratings success over its entire run, but it's also lily-white until its final year.

It's also the highest-rated locally produced program in the country. In the mid-'50s, Buddy Deane's a Baltimore radio import out of Pine Bluff, Arkansas. His radio patter is strictly mayonnaise and his ratings so-so. But he supplements his pay every weekend by running teenage dance hops. He's playing the standard pop songs of the day when he makes a discovery.

The kids aren't asking for Eddie Fisher, who sings "Oh, My Papa." They're asking for Bill Haley and the Comets, who sing "Rock Around the Clock" and Little Richard, who sings "Tutti-Fruitti."

Deane had no taste for this—he's a throwback to the big band era—but he's smart enough to see the future and slick enough to make the change from radio to TV. Instantly, he makes another discovery: kids love to watch other kids.

These Baltimore teenagers become home town heroes. The show becomes an afternoon tribal ritual for thousands of kids who race home from school to watch other kids doing the latest dance steps while wearing the trendiest fashions. The regulars on the show are known as The Committee. They become such familiar household names that, decades later, an entire generation in Baltimore still remembers them.

And somebody, after watching Boogie dance at some recreation center, or maybe out at the Dixie Ballroom at Gwynn Oak Park, or maybe the Famous Ballroom, invites him onto the show, where he's a hit.

"Well, I was always winning dance contests of one kind or another," he recalls. "So they invite me on the Buddy Deane Show, and I was such a good dancer, they invited me back. They asked me if I'd come back every day, Monday to Friday. I said, 'I have a problem. The program starts at 3. How am I gonna get over there when I don't get out of school until 3?'"

He goes to Rabbi Ephraim Shapiro, who's the principal at Talmudical Academy and naturally recalls Boogie—"Label"— from his days there. He knows this kid's no threat to become a physicist. He barely bothers to show up. When he flunked a grade at Garrison Junior High, they not only held him back— they pushed him back an entire year. He needs an outlet for all that energy, and needs something to feel good about himself.

Rabbi Shapiro convinces Milton Dickman, principal at Garrison Junior High School, to let Boogie out early.

"It changed my life," he says. "I became very popular through that show. I think I was the only Jewish kid they had. Maybe this one short little girl. But teens who were young and shy, they saw me, and they saw my moves."

The slow dances, any galumph could handle. The fast stuff, that's where you showed off.

"I had a unique move, where I held the girl's hand while I twirled her," he recalls, still picturing moments when his life began to turn. "I'd take my right leg and kick it over my hand and turn my back to her, and then I'd switch hands and turn all the way around, and sometimes pull her through my legs. I started it. Others copied it later. Typical turn, but then the right leg, and still holding hands, and then bend down and grab and pull through."

It's enough to ruin any but the sturdiest sacroiliac. But all of this gave him a sense of celebrity and, for a lifetime, a sense of ease with women. He wasn't afraid to approach them—and, when they saw him dance, some were interested enough to approach him.

The jitterbugging also helped create a nickname that lasts forever and defines an approach to life: Boogie.

He's fearless. What's he got to lose? He pursues the prettiest girls, breaks the most suffocating social rules of the era, and trades punches with obnoxious guys no matter their size.

"I remember one time," says Donald Saiontz. He's a retired Baltimore attorney who's known Boogie since junior high school. "We're in our teens, we're over at the Hilltop Shopping Center, outside of Mandell's Deli. Bunch of drapes come by."

Drapes are Bawlamerese for those '50s kids the rest of the country called greasers. They wore black leather jackets with the collars up and had their hair slicked back like jet streams. Their biggest dream in life was getting visiting privileges at some gas station grease pit.

"And they're looking for a fight, a car load of them," says Saiontz. "Couple of them jumped out of the car, and they're grabbing some of the Jewish guys. Boogie jumps right in. Went right after them. They're running off, and he's yelling, 'Come on, we gotta get after them.' He was happy to fight, and I was happy just to get safely across the street.

"But that's how he was. He was skinny, he wasn't big, but he was for real. Never had a nickel in his pocket. I know, sometimes, he didn't have food to eat. It was awful in that sense. So I guess he realized, he's gotta fight for everything. And the truth is, every time he fought, he got a little more famous around northwest Baltimore."

And not just northwest Baltimore.

He's bounced through a few high schools around town by the time he's in his junior year. This is at Baltimore City College now. In the fall of 1961, Allan Charles is a sophomore there, a kid so skinny he's known as Stick. He's hanging out at lunchtime with a couple of friends. Some big drape comes over, grabs one of Charles' pals by the necktie he's wearing and then punches him in the face. There's blood coming out of his nose, and now the drape's tossing out some serious anti-Jew language. He's got buddies behind him laughing and cheering him on.

"Believe me," Charles says, "these were not guys who'd sit around the rabbi's office studying their maftir."

In adulthood, Charles will create one of the most successful advertising and public relations firms in Baltimore. He'll handle Merry-Go-Round's TV spots once the clothing chain's ready to expand. At this time, though, Charles is "about five-feet-four, and maybe I'm 123 pounds. In my whole career at City, I went oh-for-12 in fights. But I go after this guy."

He's screaming, he's in the guy's face, he's threatening to kill him. And the bluff works.

"I don't want to fight you," the drape says, embarrassing himself in front of his pals.

This is a triumphant moment for Charles, as far as it goes. It turns out, though, these drapes have lots of friends, including some varsity football players. Charles is walking just off school grounds the next day, and a couple of big shots on the football team are hollering some more choice anti-Jew material at him. They heard about the previous day's embarrassment. They threaten to take him apart if they find Charles a little further from school grounds.

When Charles tells this story to a friend, the friend says, "You gotta go see Boogie."

"You have to understand," says Charles, "I knew who he was. Everybody knew who Boogie was, but I didn't actually know him, and he don't know me from Adam. So I go looking for him down in the school cafeteria. And it's like a scene out of 'The Godfather.' Boogie's sitting there holding court like Don Corleone. He's dishing out favors.

"I go up, I tell him the story, the whole thing about the Jew remarks, and I tell him, 'I think these guys are gonna kill me.' He says, 'I'll help you out. Don't worry.' Next day we see these guys. I'm telling you, must have been 30 of them, although as we get older Boogie claims there weren't that many. But there's a lot of them, including some football players.

"We walk up to them. Boogie's got his arm around my shoulder. He says, 'I understand you guys called my friend a dirty Jew.' From somewhere in this crowd of guys, I hear somebody say, 'Hey, man, that's Boogie.' Everybody else, there's dead silence. I'm thinking I'm gonna die right here. Then I hear another guy kinda whisper, 'Don't fuck with him.'

"And Boogie says to these guys, 'Listen to me, you mother fuckers. I hear one more word about this dirty Jew shit, and I'm gonna slap every one of you mother fuckers six feet under the fuckin' ground.' There's not a sound. We turn and walk away. And I never heard another word out of these guys, never another peep. And that's how I met Boogie Weinglass."

By the time Boogie's in high school—beginning at Forest Park, concluding at City but with intermittent stops elsewhere along the way—he's famous for fighting, and for ball playing. He's a star on the basketball court, and a starter on Forest Park's baseball team. He's not very big for basketball—never quite reaches five-feet-11 inches—but he's quick, he can jump, and he's unafraid to drive into a forest of taller players.

So, all over northwest Baltimore by now, not everybody knows Boogie—but his legend's begun to spread. Including the part about fighting.

Harold Goldsmith knows all of this when he sees Boogie come to the top of the stairs at Benny's one afternoon when they're both in high school. Harold's coming apart.

"Boogie, Boogie, would you help me?" he says.

Boogie doesn't even know this kid, but Harold knows him, because who doesn't? Harold hasn't had his growth spurt yet, and he's a little bit nerdy. He bet this drape, some Neanderthal named Shane, that he could beat him in pool, and now Shane won't pay him the money he owes him. Five bucks, maybe ten, pretty big money around 1960.

There's something in Harold's tone, the sheer plaintive cry of an injustice that's been committed, that appeals to Boogie. As they walk slowly across the room, Harold points to the guy.

He's taller than Boogie, and wiry. Boogie's not cautious, exactly, but he's inexplicably polite as he approaches the guy.

"Excuse me," he says, "but why don't you pay this guy his…"

That's about as far as he gets.

"Why don't you go fuck yourself, Jewboy," Shane says.

Now it's maybe 60 years later, but Boogie can still describe what follows, since it begins to remove him from the ranks of the impoverished.

"He's maybe six-feet-one, and I'm about five-feet-seven at the time, so I can't throw the punch straight out, I have to go up. And, as soon as he opens his mouth like that, I hit him flush in the face. He put both his hands up to his mouth, and I drop him with a left. He goes down, and I get on top of him."

Everybody in the pool room gathers around, and somebody tries to pull Boogie off this overmatched creep while punches are still being thrown. "No, no," somebody else hollers, "let Boogie kill him."

Instead, he takes the guy's pants pocket and rips it open. "He had $80 on him," Boogie still remembers, "three twenties and a couple of tens. I gave Harold his money. A bunch of guys are watching the whole thing."

Then he hears Benny's voice.

"Jesus Christ, I just let you back in the fuckin' place," he says. "You're barred for three months."

"The thing is," Boogie recalls, "Benny threw me out for fighting one time right before this. This was only my second day back."

So he walks out of the pool hall, down the stairs, with Harold right behind him. They've never even met before this, but right now Harold's like the world's most loyal cocker spaniel.

"How'd you learn to fight like that?" he asks.

The two of them are standing there on Reisterstown Road, and Boogie's not thinking about that, he's just wondering how to get home. Fortunately, Harold has a car that's parked right there. He's 16, he's just gotten his license, and to mark the occasion his family's bought him a brand new convertible.

"You need a ride?" Harold says.

They start driving, and Boogie's not sure where they're going. But it's all right, it's a nice day and a nice new car. The two of them start comparing backgrounds. Harold comes from a little money. His father owns a bunch of low-rent properties, mostly rented to black people.

In Baltimore at this time, there is so little trust white people have in blacks that rent is not collected monthly, but week by week. In the case of the Goldsmith properties, it's now falling on Harold to collect rents on these places. It's not an appealing prospect.

"Would you like to make some extra money?" Harold asks.

"Doing what?"

"Me and my father have some rentals. We rent them to shvartzes," a Yiddish word translated explicitly as "black" but carrying unsavory nuance. "You go around, and you collect the rent."

"Sure, I'll do that," Boogie says.

By this time, as they're driving through town, Boogie notices the streets are looking familiar. They're down in west Baltimore. They're on the same block where his family used to live. How do you like this, they're pulling up at Boogie's old house, 2207 Baker Street.

"Here's your first one," Harold says.

"What do you mean?"

"That house," says Harold. He's pointing to 2209.

"I lived next door," Boogie says. He's a little embarrassed that this rich kid sees how he once lived. But not so embarrassed that he doesn't get right out of the car and march up to the front door at 2209.

"Hi," the man of the house says.

"Hi," says Boogie. He gestures toward the car, where Harold has neither emerged nor turned off the engine. "You owe Mr. Goldsmith some rent." His tone is not neighborly. The man in the doorway is sufficiently anxious.

"I can give you ten dollars."

"The rent's twenty-five."

"Hold on, that's all I got."

"When can you get the rest?"

"Next week."

"And so," says Boogie, "that's how we hooked up. I went to work for Harold, collecting rents in rough neighborhoods while Harold sat in the car with the motor running."

This was a nice sideline for a kid fighting his way out of poverty. Now he could attach it to some upcoming means of employment, running football pools and selling blank report cards to schoolmates who have a little money.

Chapter Four

Diner Days and Nights

It's easy enough to get from Benny's Poolroom to the Hilltop Diner. It all depends on the mode of transportation. Those with cars navigate the eight blocks up Reisterstown Road in roughly three minutes, even in the constant traffic. Those lacking automobile comfort have been known to race on foot between the two joints, usually while clothed, but not necessarily.

One time, past midnight, and some of the diner wise guys are looking for something more than a bet. They want a memory as well. Everybody knows Boogie can run like a bandit, but so can this other kid who wants to race him.

"Who are you, Roger Bannister?"

"No, *you* are."

The usual sarcasm. Bannister just broke the four-minute mile. So, big deal, a foot race. Now they're taking bets that these two won't do it completely naked. It's Boogie who makes the suggestion, no big deal to him since he's done this for money on a few previous occasions. There's no dare he won't take, and nothing on which he won't wager. But this is one of the city's busier streets, not exactly deserted even at this hour, with the all-night diner and the late-night Mandell & Ballow's Deli directly across the street and people rather likely to take notice.

"So you were completely nude?" somebody asks Boogie many years later.

"Not completely," he says.

"Ah. So what clothes were you wearing?"

"Sneakers," he says.

The race was a dead heat, so who knows where all that money went. The point is, it was a time of looking for the smile, and often finding it, and enhancing it with the element of making a few bucks.

"It was just a bunch of guys goofing off," Barry Levinson remembered years later. Like the late-night Gene Modell race. "Yeah, I was there for that," Levinson says. "A lot of us were there."

Modell bet everybody he could run a mile in under 10 minutes. At the diner, everybody ridiculed this, and then money started changing hands. In "Diner," Modell's played by Paul Reiser. The real Modell took on all bets, and about 20 guys jumped into cars and drove all the way down to the Johns Hopkins University track to see if he could do it.

Understand, it's three in the morning, and they've been hanging out all night at the diner. Modell has a plan. He wants to cut down on wind resistance, so he takes off his shirt and then, what the hell, his pants. He's down to his jockey undershorts. He beat the ten-minute mark by two seconds and collapsed across the finish line with guys cheering him like it's the Preakness.

"The whole thing made sense at the time," Levinson says. "But I have no idea why."

"It was a smile," says the attorney Donald Saiontz. "That's all."

The Hilltop Diner's full of people stretching the laughs as long as possible. Levinson's youthful cast in "Diner," for example, the ones like Boogie and Fenwick and Modell - they're caught between adolescence and adulthood and don't particularly want to be either.

They're a new kind of Hollywood version of Jews. This is not "Exodus" or "The Pawnbroker" or "Gentleman's Agreement." These are nobody's victims, not any more. They're smart aleck Americans who just happen to be Jewish. They're as wise-ass as any Italian Catholic or Irish Protestant.

In real life, they're the first generation of Jews whose parents made it out of the white inner city's cramped little row houses all the way out to tract homes with finished basements and grassy back yards and nearby all-night hangouts like the Hilltop Diner to replace front stoops as gathering spots.

At the diner, people sit there kibitzing all night long. They're not all Jews, but a lot of them are. They might be descendants of rabbis and scholars, but now these smart alecks are staging modern cultural debates: Who would you rather make out with, Marilyn Monroe or Brigitte Bardot? Who's cooler, Elvis or Bobby Darin? Who's the better quarterback, Johnny Unitas, or...? Oh, please, somebody shut this fool up.

Among the diner's scattered teenage tribes, there's a whole bunch of guys who will make it big somewhere down the road. Levinson, of course, becomes Hollywood legend. Richard Sher co-hosts a TV talk show for nearly a decade with a young woman named Oprah Winfrey. Kenny Waisman becomes a Broadway producer and re-invents the era with a show called "Grease." Jay Tarses gets big in sitcom TV. There's one teenage cherub everybody here calls Benjy. He becomes U.S. Senator Benjamin Cardin.

Then we have the future Merry-Go-Round duo, Goldsmith and Boogie. Among this crowd, neither is remotely suspected of future cultural greatness.

Harold's got money coming in from his father's slum properties, but who wants to spend a lifetime collecting rent in tough neighborhoods? Smart guy, but completely anal. Jan Abrams remembers taking out a cigarette one night at the diner and realizing he didn't have a match.

"Harold," he said, "you got a light?"

Harold took out a pack and started counting.

"I've got 17 cigarettes and 17 matches," he said. "So I can't give you a match."

"You're kidding."

"No, I'm not," Harold said.

Among the diner guys, Harold's not exactly an insider. "He couldn't even make parking lot," said Danny Snyder. It's Snyder's way of saying Goldsmith was lucky to get in the front door, much less crowd his way in to sit with the cool guys.

Harold's hyper as hell, and he's got a gnat's attention span. His head's with you, and then it's not. Somebody gave him a nickname: Oliver, or Ollie. It's meant to indicate he's a little bit fussy.

"Harold was the adult person," Barry Levinson recalls. "We were half idiots, and he was like an adult. If we were all screwing around, with nothing to do, talking about girls and stuff, none of that applied to Harold. He'd talk about serious stuff. When I think about him teaming up with Boogie—well, it's an odd coupling. You couldn't have found two people more different than those two."

Within the diner crowd, though, neither's a perfect fit. Harold's so damned serious. And Boogie's not one for sitting around bullshitting all night. Sometimes he's out on the parking lot, or he's across the street outside Mandell's Deli. Maybe he's checking the odds on some ballgame, placing a small bet, ducking in and out of the diner, sweet-talking some girl. It all depends on his impulse of the moment.

They're all perfecting the art of the hang-out. If they've got a Saturday night date and they're driving past the diner and see familiar cars parked out front, they have a choice: pray they can get to second base with the young lady, which is a long shot, or drop her off early and head back to the diner for guaranteed knock sessions. This being the 1950s, they naturally drop off their dates. And, endlessly, they talk about the Baltimore Colts, who are the town's great secular religion and its binding spirit.

This is summed up in the confession uttered by Donald Saiontz, who spent his adolescence at the diner. Decades later, still vividly recalling those nights, he says, "There were only two topics of conversation at the Hilltop Diner. The Colts, and sex. And usually it was the Colts, because you didn't have to lie about them."

But, sex aside, there's something liberating in the post-war years. The old gentrified bigotries are looking less fashionable since the war. The Jews, always cautious, feel a growing sense of acceptance. They're feeling a little more Americanized than they've ever felt before. In this moment stretching from the Ike-and-Mamie White House years through Kennedy's Camelot, maybe it's time to step out of the old ethnic ghettos and get a broader piece of the city's public life.

Some of this is reflected in who's showing up at the diner for a little high-profile schmoozing, traipsing among the noisy, crowded tables and booths, and the cigarette smoke and the waitresses with their mile-a-minute patter.

There's Hyman Pressman, composing instant doggerel upon any request. Pressman's the city comptroller, watchdog over all municipal spending. He also knocks off good-natured lines about anything from presidential politics to the opening of a bagel emporium. Here he is, celebrating his own election and the mayoral victory of Tommy D'Alesandro III:

Tommy will make a wonderful skipper

Lady Luck's with him, and he won't trip her.

If things go wrong

We won't worry long

We'll just fast during Lent and Yom Kippur.

Not far from Pressman, there's Irv Kovens holding court. He sits there behind a big un-lit cigar. Over at his store in west Baltimore, he sells furniture on the installment plan, mostly in black neighborhoods, and then his salesmen knock on doors every week to collect. It's a variation on the job Boogie's doing, in his teens, while jittery Harold waits in the car with the motor running. Collect the money and get away quickly.

But furniture's just a business for Kovens. His real passion is politics. He'll become one of the king makers of his era. He's the man behind Spiro Agnew, who becomes Richard Nixon's vice president (and later resigns in disgrace) and Marvin Mandel, who becomes governor of Maryland (and later goes to prison, along with Kovens) and William Donald Schaefer, who becomes mayor of Baltimore and then governor of Maryland.

But it's not only big shots and kids who are diner regulars. Here are "tin men" who hustle aluminum siding all day, horse players who show up after a hard day's wagering at nearby Pimlico Race Course, mothers arriving after P-TA meetings, bowlers who just rolled some duckpins around the corner at the Hilltop Lanes, folks emerging from a Cinemascope movie at the Crest theater across the street, and all those bit players arriving after meetings at Jack Pollack's nearby Trenton Democratic

Club, where everybody begs Boss Pollack to get their traffic tickets fixed by a few friendly downtown judges.

Pollack precedes Irv Kovens as political king maker. During Prohibition, Pollack made a living as an enforcer for bootleggers. He gets into the insurance business, learns to quote Shakespeare to give himself a patina of class, and forms his organization, from which he runs all Jewish politics for a few decades until Kovens muscles him aside.

Then there's the "biggest" one of all in the Hilltop Diner crowd. It's Fat Earl Magid, a fulltime cab driver and part-time pool hustler who eats his way through everything. At 385 pounds, Earl barely fits into a booth. He bets on eating, and claims never to have lost. One night Earl ate 52 Little Tavern hamburgers. Another time, down in Little Italy, he ate five pounds of spaghetti and 100 meatballs, plus one and a half gallons of wine. He won fourteen hundred dollars for this. But his moment of pride came at the Hilltop Diner, with witnesses who could testify, where he ate the entire breakfast side of the menu. It was a wonderful moment, if you weren't there when Earl started digesting.

Directly across bustling Reisterstown Road from the diner there's the Hilltop Shopping Center strip mall, with Mandell and Ballow's restaurant. Anybody in northwest Baltimore who's not at the Hilltop Diner, or the Lotus Inn Chinese restaurant down the block, is hanging at Mandell's.

Mandell's shares the strip mall with Holzer's Bakery, Saler's Dairy and Scherr & Dreiband kosher butchers and half a dozen other stores. Also, with the narrow barber shop which displays magazine cutouts of unclothed female models on its men's room wall. This becomes a kind of cultural Mecca. In the great sexual wasteland of the '50s, it's the wall where many young lads first discover their previously latent hormones.

"Ma, I need a haircut," they tell their mothers on the day after they first lay eyes on the naked ladies.

"You got a haircut yesterday."

"I think I need another. Please, I love getting haircuts."

So it's a busy area on both sides of Reisterstown Road at this time, and you can find Boogie at one place or another, depending on the night. Or, sometimes, both sides on the same night.

Such as the time he's at the diner, but gets tossed out. For a change, he's gotten into a fight. He's sitting in a booth with a few pals, his voice maybe an octave too loud for some guy sitting in the next booth with his date.

He tells Boogie to keep it down.

"I may have used some profanity," Boogie recalls later. He's being coy. "Anyway, I didn't like the way he spoke to me. He came at me. He actually did, which was a big mistake. I banked him a couple of times, right there inside the diner. And the guy put his head down, and turned away, and it was over."

Among the witnesses to this was George Stamas, then in his mid-thirties, who owns the diner. One minute he's fussing in the kitchen, the next he's wiping off tables. He's there when people come for lunch, and he's still there when they're heading home at three in the morning. Some think he never goes home.

Now he says, "Okay, Boogie, get out, you're barred."

It's not the first time this has happened here. And the diner's not the only place around, as everybody knows. So Boogie instinctively crosses Reisterstown Road and walks into Mandell & Ballow's.

The place is not only packed but carries the fulsome odor of pickles and sour tomatoes, found in bowls on every table. You could feast on this alone. But Boogie makes an immediate turn inside the front door and heads down nearby steps to the men's room one floor down.

He feels the need to straighten up a little after the skirmish across the street. His hair's a little unkempt, and his clothes are the usual third-hand stuff his brothers used to wear. His mother patched the pants. Then some fraternity hot shot comes in, wearing an outfit Boogie can still describe, so deep was his antipathy then and even now.

"Ivy League outfit, necktie, loafers," he says. "Cocky guy. He was six feet, taller than me. I'm 16, and he's a year or two older. He takes one look at me and calls me a dirtball."

Boogie goes right after him. Decades after the fact, he sounds like Howard Cosell reviewing Ali-Frazier.

"Hit him right, left, he's bleeding from the nose and he's starting to drop. He grabs me in a headlock. We both go down, but I'm on top. I'm still in the headlock, but I'm hitting him in the ear. You get hit in the ear, you lose your equilibrium, you're done. Eventually, he lets go. He's half unconscious, it looks like.

"And some guy in his forties comes in, knew who I was. He goes upstairs and tells on me. It's a Friday or Saturday night, and the police always had a car or two parked between Mandell's and the Crest Theater, because there's always some kind of trouble on weekends."

Here come the police through the front door, asking what's going on. And, emerging from the basement, straightening his clothes as though he has no idea what's transpired, comes Boogie. He and the police pass in different directions. The officers go down the stairs, and Boogie hurries outside. Knowing he'd better vacate, he makes a remarkable discovery. One of the cops has left his motor running. This quickly becomes the only police vehicle in history used as a getaway car.

Boogie doesn't necessarily have a driver's license at this point in his life, and the car's a stick shift, which is a problem. He's never driven one. But never mind. "I'm completely crazy," he reflects. He gets in, and now he's driving up Reisterstown Road. But he can't figure out how to get the damned car out of first gear.

So it's jerking like crazy. He's doing 8 or 10 miles per hour. But it's a police car, so it's a smile. He sputters up to Ameche's Drive-In, which is usually packed since it's named for the great Baltimore Colts fullback.

"I gotta be seen," he thinks. So he's got a big goofy smile on his face, and he's looking for people to wave to, until sanity returns. If he gets caught, his mother will be unhappy. She'll tell big brother Jackie. Jackie will then beat hell out of him. This is standard operating procedure. So, after an hour or so, Boogie has to ditch the police car and hide in his room before somebody figures out he's the culprit behind the missing vehicle.

He parks the car near home. When he walks in, Nettie sees the blood all over his shirt, left over from the fight with the fraternity punk.

"Label, what did you do?" she cries.

"Got in a fight, mom, but it's all right. This is not my blood, it's somebody else's."

He goes to sleep, only to be awakened before dawn. There's a pounding on the front door, not totally unexpected. Boogie tries to slip out the back door. The police are there, too. They take him away in handcuffs. The last words he hears are his mother's.

"Oy, vey, why you all the time fighting?"

"Not all the time, mom," he calls back to her.

True enough. When he's not fighting, he's pursuing girls, without even a trace of shyness in his personality. He's hungry for affection, for romance, for some kind of validation.

And, never to be minimized, for sex.

It's not an easy time for this. Hopeful high school boys of the era purchase Trojan condoms and carry them in their wallets as badges of sophistication. The condoms remain in almost every wallet. They remain there so long that they leave indented circles in the leather.

In this era, mothers insist that daughters remain virgins until wedding nights, or what man would possibly want them? When teenage boys compare notes on a weekend's dating triumphs, they issue front-line battle reports heavily embellished by imagination, like Vietnam body counts a decade later.

The astute writer Dan Wakefield laments, "Ours was the last generation for whom foreplay was accepted as an end in itself." In "Diner," Levinson takes it a step further. Mickey Rourke, playing Boogie, asks Eddie, (Steve Guttenberg), as he's approaching his wedding night, "You're still a virgin, aren't you?"

"Technically," Eddie replies. Meaning, as one of the guys laments, "six years of a platonic relationship."

Not for Boogie, such a life. He's not only getting laid, he's involved in closet scenes, where one lucky guy will find a spare bedroom for sex and a couple of pals will hide out in a nearby closet so they can observe the proceedings. In the movie, Boogie does the gentlemanly thing and backs out of a closet scene with the unsuspecting Ellen Barkin. In the life of some '50s adolescents, who are suffering through America's long sexual drought, the closet scene's their way of finding second-hand thrills.

But Boogie's in his own sexual zone.

If he hasn't got a girlfriend willing to go past second base (hands above the waist, unhooked bra), there's always Anna Okanka, widely known as Kank. Boogie discovers her when Kank's in the middle of her own legend. To teenage boys she's an older woman—actually, she might be 50 - and she's on the make for countless numbers of young guys across northwest Baltimore.

Boogie meets her when he's at work. He's making bicycle deliveries for one of the neighborhood pharmacies. Kank is a regular drug store customer, and it happens that she lives a few doors over from Boogie's house, Violet and Towanda avenues.

They hit it off right away. Kank is described as plain looking, unmarried, nobody's dream girl. But she welcomes all comers. Handfuls of guys line up at her place all the time. Reliable reports say the leader of a local boys club sometimes parks his car outside her house to make certain none of his lads sully themselves at Kank's. But, for many teenage boys, this is their sexual initiation, and their brief liberation from the era's sexual wasteland, as well.

And Boogie, living right in the neighborhood, becomes a pal as well as a partner. When he gets in trouble at home, he hangs out at Kank's. Trouble at school, which can lead to trouble at home, he stays at Kank's. They fulfill each other's various needs, here and there.

But he's got serious girlfriends, as well. His mother keeps tabs on them, and always wants to know two things: are they Jewish; and, has the girl's father got any money?

One time, he's dating Stephanie Horn, whose father, Emanuel Horn, is a well-known local attorney and hates Boogie. Stephanie's 16. Boogie's 19. He's got possession of his brother Jackie's car for the evening since Jackie took an early nap and Boogie swiped his car keys as Jackie slept.

"We're sitting at Ameche's Drive-in," he recalls. "I'm ordering from the car. Our windows are down. Couple of rednecks in the next car, one of them says something. Some Jew remark, something about my nose. My nose was so big, and my face wasn't filled in yet. Wasn't hard to see I was Jewish.

"So I get out of the car and he gets out, and I beat the shit out of him. I've got him down on the ground. The other guy gets out of the car, sees I beat up his friend, and he runs the other way.

"So management at Ameche's calls the police. I'm back sitting in the car with Stephanie, waiting for our hamburgers, and the police ask for my license. The rednecks are gone by now. The police arrest me. One reason, I didn't actually have a driver's license."

The cops take the two of them, Stephanie and Boogie, straight down Reisterstown Road maybe half a mile, about midway between the Hilltop Diner and Benny's Pool Room, to the Northwest District Police Station.

Boogie's now behind bars. Stephanie's waiting around for her father, the distinguished attorney, to pick her up. The police all know Emmanuel Horn, as he's often represented clients in the Northwest District courtroom, located in this same building just behind the desk sergeant's domain.

Horn walks in, sees his daughter, and asks the nearest officer, "Where's the young man?" He's escorted back to the lockup area. He stands just outside Boogie's cell, as close as he can get to this miscreant. He's like a gawker at the lion's cage at the Baltimore Zoo. He's warned his daughter, over and over, stay away, this kid's no good. And here's the proof.

"If I ever catch you with my daughter again," he says, wagging his index finger all the way through the bars of the cell, "I'll break every bone…"

Boogie's not about to listen to this, not when he figures he's done nothing wrong. He grabs Horn's index finger. He won't let go. Horn's trying to get away, and Boogie's twisting and bending. Horn's erupting in rage and pain.

"I wasn't gonna let go," Boogie recalls. "I was a rough, crazy kid, and I didn't like how he was talking to me."

The police have to liberate Horn's index finger. Then they politely suggest he go home. As for the great romance, it was over for about three months. "And then Stephanie started sneaking out," says Boogie. "She was one of my first loves."

But not his last.

There comes a time when he meets his future wife, the first of Boogie's three marriages. Joanie Sutton was 15, meaning she was in 10th grade; Boogie was 19, which means he was in the 11th. The numbers may seem skewed, but they're precise.

Now it's a Friday night dance at the Milford Mill quarry. "Some slow dancing going on, and Joanie's with some guy," Boogie remembers. "But I catch her eye. I go over and tap the guy on the shoulder to break in. He made a big mistake. He shoved me out of the way."

Seconds later, the poor guy's on the floor. There's a bouncer who sees this, and throws Boogie out of the place, "and don't come back." Boogie leaves, but he lingers on the parking lot for a while with Barry Levinson and a few other pals. And here comes a car, moving pretty fast.

"Two guys in the car, and one of them points at me," Boogie says. "It's the older brother of the guy I beat up. He found a pay phone and made a call. Here he comes at me. I figure I'm all ready for him, but he pulls out a switch blade, a long one. I never had a guy pull a switchblade on me before."

Barry Levinson remembers it vividly, and wonders even now if the fight involved ethnic differences, no matter that it started over a mere dance.

"There was always a little bit of friction between Jews and gentiles back then," Levinson says. "A friction. I think that added to the atmosphere. And now there's a small crowd that's gathered around the two of them, and the guy pulls out this blade.

"Instead of Boogie going, 'Oh, my God,' the way most people would, he looks at the guy and says, 'What is this, comic books?' Everybody laughed, including the guy, who glances around the crowd. And, in the flash of a second the guy's on the ground and Boogie's pounding him. He had absolutely no fear."

The knife did a little damage, though.

"I'm leaning on the hood of a Chevy Impala," Boogie recalls. "He cuts me pretty good, draws a little blood on my stomach. But I grabbed his wrist, and that was that. I wouldn't let go. When you're up against a knife, you're real strong. We go down, I'm on top of him, and I banged his wrist on the concrete. I grabbed the knife and flung it, and then I really kicked the crap out of him. And, after that, I just started stalking Joanie."

All this, and he's still got the remainder of high school to navigate.

Chapter Five

Class Distinctions

On that bright September morning Boogie Weinglass first arrives at Forest Park High School, he counts the house and calculates the odds. At this time, about three-quarters of all Forest Park students are female. In each precious face, he sees potential for love and romance and, nearly as crucial, wide-open shots at copying off some smart girl's test paper.

The girls are mostly cooperative, but teachers are not. The phrase that lingers in his ears after all these years is, "Eyes on your own paper, Weinglass." He believes no one ever developed such a long neck as his, from stretching out to see somebody else's answers.

He arrives at Forest Park a little late, owing to his junior high school record, which exceeded the normal three years. Did it take four years, or five? It's a little fuzzy, but the history is clear that he started at Garrison Junior High and finished at Pimlico Junior High, amid a flurry of warnings and after-school sessions and suspensions.

At Forest Park, there was the usual mischief, except for those days when he simply neglected to show up. Then, if he did check in for a cameo appearance, he'd still skip a class here and there. He's always off playing ball, or placing a bet, or looking for a new hustle. It helps that Knocko's Poolroom is pretty close to the school, so he doesn't have to go all the way over to Benny's. But all of this leads to resounding academic failure.

In retrospect, there's a certain inevitability: Yiddish in the home, Hebrew in the Talmudical Academy schooling where English was regarded as a "foreign" language. And then the plunge into public school. Could he speak English? Yes, of course. He'd been running the streets his whole life. But, anything on the printed page, he's been stranded far behind his new public school classmates.

What's all this brand new talk about parsing sentences, about adverbs and modifiers and split infinitives? And who cares about irregular French verbs or the opposite angles of parallelograms? What in the world do such things have to do with real life?

Not a thing in this kid's world. And so he makes his own rules, defies authority figures with sly bravura, or comic wink, or blithe indifference. His classmates want to toe the line, that's their problem. He'll make his own way.

"Put it this way, I wasn't an English major," he says. "I didn't know from sentences, I didn't know from commas. It was real frustrating. And I was insecure from the other stuff, like being poor and dressing bad. And I over-reacted to all of it."

When he finally gets to Forest Park, maybe two-thirds of the students are middle class Jewish kids academically primed from the start by doting parents. It's the post-war golden age of Jewish academic stardom, when the snobby prestige colleges—including the nearby Johns Hopkins University—are finally easing their shameful quotas on Jews and other minorities.

These Forest Park kids know what's expected of them. Check any classroom, this is a generation where they're dutifully memorizing the dates of major Civil War battles, they're carrying around slide rules in their shirt pockets, they're reading Hemingway and Fitzgerald, they're mixing things that bubble inside chemistry test tubes. If they're feeling real rebellious, they're reading "Catcher in the Rye." Their parents may have been cheated by the depression and the war, but these are the baby boomers who will march off to their fullest potential.

Boogie, however, barely bothers carrying a notebook to school. What's the point of it when he's already so far behind in so many ways?

And it's not just school. His classmates are fully embracing the era's adolescent culture, while Boogie's outside peering through the window. He can see, but he can't reach. And this gnaws at his subconscious, and then expresses itself impulsively.

The kids at Forest Park are post-war conspicuous consumers. They're buying 45s of the young Elvis Presley, often played on some brand new stereo hi-fi record player. Boogie's family is happy they finally have a home telephone. These kids' families mirror TV's "Father Knows Best." Boogie hardly sees his father by this time. The Forest Park kids have enough money from their parents to go clothes shopping each new season. Boogie sees his own clothes as signals that he doesn't belong.

In this crowded little era, Forest Park turns out a whole bunch of future high achievers - doctors, lawyers, scientists— and quite a few public figures. There's Levinson, who will head for Hollywood and the movies. There's Ellen Cohen, who becomes Cass Elliott and sings with the Mamas and the Papas. There's Billy Griffin, future Motown member of The Miracles. And Ken Waissman, who will produce such Broadway hits as "Grease," which makes the entire country long for a return to the '50s. There's Jay Tarses, who will create TV's "Buffalo Bill" and "Days and Nights of Molly Dodd." And David Jacobs, who will create TV's "Dallas" and "Knots Landing."

Amid such achievers, Boogie needs a way to distract everybody from his own shortcomings. So he acts out. He's known to throw a nasty sucker punch. He's known to shout across a crowded auditorium, "Your sister's a whore," in the middle of a speech by the student government president. He becomes a symbol of the rebel inside every teenage boy.

But sports gives him his first legitimate respect.

"School was not exactly his area," Barry Levinson says, understating only by light years. "He couldn't sit still, and didn't care. He was an outsider who everybody knew. But we didn't know everything."

The worst of it, Boogie can set aside when he steps onto a basketball court or a baseball field. In both sports, he earns starting varsity positions his first year. He's following his brother Jackie in sports. Jackie was a baseball star at Forest Park. Hit the hell out of the ball, and he'd have guys hit him grounders by the hour. Some guys, big league scouts included, saw some serious potential.

Boogie doesn't quite have Jackie's respect for rules. Some days, he does nothing but play ball. He cuts an entire day of classes and shows up at game time. Some days, he cuts maybe the morning classes, claims he was busy helping his mother, and drops in for a few afternoon classes and then plays ball.

In the history of high school sports, this is an odd moment.

These are the early years of integration in Baltimore's schools, including the playing fields. In the late '50s, we're only heartbeats since America's youth are permitted to sit in the same public school classrooms, regardless of skin color. For about a dozen years, there arrives a legitimate mix of black youngsters with whites.

It takes a little longer for the schools' sports leagues to integrate.

Yes, the Supreme Court ended legalized public school segregation in 1954. But it's somehow taken the city schools' ruling athletic board, the Maryland Scholastic Association, another three years before they allow the historically black schools to compete with the historically white. Heaven forbid, precious white boys should sweat under the same backboards with the colored youth of Dunbar, Carver and Douglass high schools.

The shadow of race hangs over everything. The schools of the city of Baltimore are quick to integrate, but a year after the Supreme Court ruling, 14 Maryland counties out of 22 were still segregated. It takes three years for Harford County to integrate, and three years before 78 schools in Baltimore County finally integrate. And it's eight years after the high court's decision before the last five Maryland counties open their doors to black students.

As the schools and their surrounding neighborhoods struggle to adjust, here come the hungry realtors and the moving vans, and the politicians who play on people's fears, and the white clergy who stand by and remain silent. The message everywhere is clear: If you leave the city, you won't have to worry about your precious white child having to mix with any of these riffraff black children. And all of this sets off a second suburban exodus since the war's end.

When Boogie arrives at Forest Park for 10th grade, it's 1958 and he's about to turn 17. The school has about fifteen hundred students. Fewer than a hundred are black. But by the end of that tumultuous decade, almost all whites will be gone, including those from the school's surrounding neighborhoods.

In the midst of all this change, Boogie's rolling with the punches—sometimes, literally. He spends his summers at Douglass High School, historically all black—where he's got to make up all those subjects he flunked during the regular school year.

"I had a few fights there," he says, "but I became friendly with the fullback on Douglass's football team. He saw me fighting in the hall with some kid, and he protected me. Not many guys bothered me after that."

For a while, he's got a black girlfriend. When they walk together, they hold hands. In Baltimore at this time, inter-racial dating can provoke heart attacks on both sides. Start with this girl's parents. They're both doctors, and they're united in their evaluation of the daughter's choice of young men. They hate Boogie, even when the daughter explains that his real name is Leonard. But the romance, brief as it is, is a signal to all: Boogie goes his own way.

The relationship fades on its own accord, as happens in youth. The real teenage triumphs for Boogie come with sports.

In basketball, he's a ball of fire. He's quick, he can jump, and he's not afraid to drive into a crowd of defenders who tower over him. He's been doing this since he was a youngster and the big guys on the playground wanted him on their teams.

In baseball, he's equally aggressive. Forest Park's got a pitcher named Don Gallon, who later does pretty well in the Baltimore Orioles farm system. Boogie's his catcher. Gallon's got an intimidating fastball. The high school games only go seven innings and, in one game, Gallon strikes out 18 batters out of 21.

"When I was catching him," Boogie recalls, "I'd call for a fastball high and inside on the first pitch of the game. They'd have their foot in the bucket the rest of the day."

But it's basketball where he stands out. Partly, it's because Boogie's good; partly, because the rest of the team's pretty bad.

"It's because we didn't have any black guys," he says. "And the one or two we did have couldn't jump. I could out-rebound all of them. One time, we played City College and lost by 30 points." This, at a time when high school teams averaged less than 50 points a game. "To this day, it's the most humiliating game I ever played in."

But not the most contentious.

There's an intrasquad scrimmage one afternoon in the school gym. There's only nine guys, so the jayvee coach, Jerry Phipps, will play just to even the sides. Phipps is a young guy. He's only a few years out of Western Maryland College, where he lettered in baseball, basketball, and football. He's slender, but he's tough. And he's guarding Boogie.

"I go in for a layup," Boogie recalls, "and I go around Phipps. He tried to stop me. He hit my thighs. When I came down, I landed on my back. My head also hit. I was down for a little bit."

When he got up, he says, he went after Phipps. "Not many guys in high school do that," meaning tangle physically with a teacher, "but I had that quick fuse. We went to the floor together."

Maybe it was a fight, maybe just a quick scrap. It's tough to tell after so many years. Cooler heads quickly separate the two of them, but the incident will be recorded in the school principal's office, in the official folder already brimming with the usual Weinglass violations.

When Nettie learns of such incidents, she's distressed enough to pass this information to eldest son Jackie, who's six years older than Boogie. Jackie will take it out on his brother by throwing him against a wall or slapping him around. This is their brotherly pattern. Jackie's generally protective of his youngest brother, but when the occasion arises, he's the designated tough guy.

Boogie will avoid such confrontations by carefully hanging out for a day or two at Kank's house down the block.

One thing the Forest Park administration does not seem to know about is a little matter of hot-wiring cars. One of Boogie's teachers, female, arrives each morning and never leaves until the end of the school day. No lunchtime dining out for her. She leaves her car in the teacher's parking area, where it stays.

Boogie takes note of this, and hot-wires her car on days he wishes to leave school grounds. Sometimes he and a few pals just drive around, and sometimes they spin over to Knocko's Pool Room at Liberty Heights Avenue and Garrison Boulevard, before returning the car to its reserved spot.

Is this wrong? Of course. Is it malicious? Not precisely, since he figures no one will ever know about it. No harm, no foul. He operates with the blithe approach, as he does with most things, that it's a smile, nothing more, so where's the problem?

This is going pretty well, and no authority figure seems any the wiser.

But now comes early spring of Boogie's second year at Forest Park. He's feeling a little ticked off, for reasons now blurred, at the baseball coach, Andy Anderson. Forget baseball, Boogie says, he'll go out for track this spring.

He's training to run the mile. He's so serious, he runs up to five miles a day, and finishes up with wind sprints. He wants to show Anderson he doesn't need baseball. Also, there's a meet scheduled between Forest Park's high school kids and the track team at Johns Hopkins University. Hopkins has a hotshot miler named Wagner, and Boogie wants to beat him.

"In my whole life," he says, "I never worked so hard at anything. I was gonna make a name for myself, because everybody knew Wagner was the best miler around. This is my dream, to beat Wagner."

The dream dies two days before the meet.

It's lunchtime at Forest Park, and Boogie's decided to leave campus. He gets the usual idea. He'll slip over to the parking lot and hot-wire that teacher's car while nobody's looking. What the hell, she never goes out for lunch, so she'll never know.

Except, this time, the lady decides to go out somewhere.

"For some reason, I didn't want to eat in the cafeteria that day," Boogie remembers. "So I borrowed the car, which I'd been doing pretty regularly for about a month. I hot-wired it, which was easy. All you had to do was put the car in neutral, get the aluminum foil from a cigarette pack, and put it around those four wires that come down which aren't housed in anything. They're hard plastic with some flexibility."

He does this with a couple of other delinquents, Wayne Smith and Tommy O'Toole. "Couple of gentiles," he says. "I gravitated to rough guys, who tended to be goyim. Anyway, the three of us go off somewhere, and we bring it right back when we're done. And she's there, the teacher."

And not only the teacher, but two city cops.

"Why did you steal this?" one of them inquires.

"I didn't really steal it," Boogie says. "It's more like borrowing."

He's explaining the distinction when the cops put all three of the lads in handcuffs and march them away.

It's Boogie's last day at Forest Park. Whatever chance he had to beat the great miler Wagner is now gone. Whatever happened to his co-defendants in the car swiping, who knows? But Boogie's expelled, never in this lifetime to come back.

By now, it's become clear that some of the wilder aspects of his life are catching up to him. Others spend their summers at the beach, or overnight camps, or simply loll around the house. He spends his vacation time in summer school, catching up on subjects he's failed.

"I never cared about marks," he says. "I was just trying to pass a grade."

But, as failure arrives, he realizes that some of his friends may be younger, but they're passing him by. Some are moving on to college, which feels distant as the Milky Way. And he's digging a hole into the earth.

Chapter Six

An Invading Army of One

Permanently banished from Forest Park High School, Boogie goes nowhere for the next six months except maybe Benny's and the Hilltop Diner. He's flunked so many classes, he can't even get into summer school. So he sits out until the following fall, when he enters Baltimore City College for a second attempt at his junior year. He's about to be 19 years old.

City is known in song and legend as the Castle on the Hill. The building sits majestically on 33rd Street like some impregnable fortress with a stone tower. From such a height, it's easy to imagine ancient kings hurling down molten lead at invading armies.

Boogie's about to be an invading army of one.

The school, all male at this time, produces those who make history. Three of its graduates will serve in the U.S. Congress—at the same time. Try finding another school in America with such a record. It's the country's third oldest public high school and welcomes young men of every background from all across the city of Baltimore. Its athletic rivalry with cross-town Polytechnic is older than Army-Navy, and equally passionate.

When new students arrive for first-day initiation each autumn, they gather in the auditorium to hear the beloved school principal, Henry T. Yost, a gentle soul with a rheumy voice and the last high-collar dress shirts in America, tell them, "Gentlemen, you have passed your first intelligence test by choosing City College as your high school." Then he adds, "The future mayor of Baltimore sits in this room right now. That is the history of Baltimore City College."

Safe to say, he is not specifically referencing Boogie Weinglass.

It's a wonder he's here at all. When he's thrown out of Forest Park the previous spring, he can't even go home. First, the cops have him. Then, when he calls his mother with the bad news about his arrest, she tells him, "Yankel's going to kill you when he hears this."

Yankel, that's Yiddish for brother Jackie. As the oldest brother, Jackie's the closest thing to a father figure. He'll slam Boogie against a wall as a fatherly gesture.

"You can't come home," Nettie warns. So, for a week, he doesn't.

He hides out at Kank's house.

Daytime, Boogie's running around town while Kank's entertaining her standard lineup of teenage lads looking to get lucky. Nights, or whenever he gets back from running the streets, Boogie's got a spot on Kank's living room sofa until brother Yankel cools off. That takes a full week.

When autumn comes, and he enters City College, Boogie does not set the world on fire. The usual misdemeanors, mostly cutting classes. But then, in a crowded second floor hallway one day, he hears some wise guy call him a name. The wise guy's full of himself, since his father owns one of the big car dealerships in town. Also, he makes a remark about Jews. Boogie nails him so hard the guy bangs his head against a wall, and he's out cold. Within the hour, Boogie's tossed out of school, and never mind what started the fight.

He winds up at Mergenthaler Tech, also known as Mervo. The school's only a few blocks from City College, but it's a different academic atmosphere. These kids are not aiming for Harvard. Eventually, they're headed for the steel mills at Sparrows Point, or the assembly lines at the GM plant on Broening Highway, or maybe they'll read meters for the gas and electric company. Perfectly respectable jobs, but Mervo's got a rougher atmosphere than the one at City.

It takes no time at all for the fighting to start at Mervo, and for Boogie to get tossed out once again.

Now, in desperation, he resorts to ethnic cliché. He gets help from his rabbi. It's his old principal at the Talmudical Academy, Rabbi Ephraim Shapiro. Years later, when Boogie's a big success written about in magazines, Jackie Weinglass will tell the Baltimore Jewish Times, "Rabbi Shapiro maintained our Yiddishkeit. He was our substitute father. He kept us in line."

A modest, sensitive man, Rabbi Shapiro understands Boogie in ways the public school people are too busy to figure out. He sees a raw kid, always in trouble, but he knows the psychological forces at play. The aggressiveness masks insecurity. The acting-out is a cry for attention. To school officials of the era, attention deficit disorder does not yet have a name. The rabbi sits down with the superintendent of the city's public schools, John Fisher. Boogie's in the room, under orders to keep quiet.

"Leonard is in school for basketball and girls, but not an education," the superintendent says. He's got Boogie's entire transcript in front of him, and it's impressive in all the wrong ways. "He doesn't care about school. He doesn't belong in our schools."

The transcript shows Boogie's history dating back through Garrison and Pimlico and Forest Park. All the fights, all the cutting up in class, all the failures. When the teachers and the principals warned about violations going on his "permanent record," they apparently meant it.

"I know him since he's a boy," the rabbi tells the superintendent. "I did his bar mitzvah. He's a smart boy, he's not dumb. He can do the work. He needs one more chance."

Finally, with apparent reluctance, Fisher says, "Tell you what I'll do. I'll let him back at City College on a trial basis. I know he wants to play basketball. Any incidents, cutting school, any fighting, there's no basketball."

"What if he makes the honor roll?" Rabbi Shapiro asks.

Now a stunned silence fills the room. The mere suggestion of academic honors provokes astonishment from everyone, including the rabbi himself.

"If he makes the honor roll," says the superintendent, "well, let's just say he'll be entitled to play. Although I doubt…"

The superintendent's words trail off, but no matter. Boogie's back in school, where he's about to find at least the beginnings of some stability. For now, walking through the halls of City College, here comes the school's new basketball coach. It's Jerry Phipps, recently transferred from Forest Park, where he was the jayvee coach and had that little intra-squad skirmish with Boogie a year ago.

Many years later, we'll find Phipps in Vero Beach, Florida. As Boogie approaches 80, Phipps passes 92. Each remembers the moment they reacquainted themselves, more than 60 years ago, in a hallway between classes at City College.

"I guess you're still mad at me," says Boogie.

"No, I'm glad you're in school," Phipps says.

"Can I come out for basketball?"

Yes, but there are provisions, says Phipps. If he misses practice, he's off the team. If he cuts class, he's off the team. If he gets into trouble, he's off the team. Phipps tells him this in the hallway, and later he brings Boogie down to the coaches' dank little dressing room, where he reinforces the message.

Phipps can be found in that room each day with all the other coaches. There's easy jock banter in there, but Phipps is found mostly reading books about basketball. He immerses himself in tactics of the great coaches of history. His first team at City won't be very good, but thereafter they'll win so many championships that Phipps will go on to coach community college teams, where he'll win even more titles. Wherever he goes, he's got his rules—not only about the game, but how to live off the court, as well.

The rules will matter to Boogie because basketball's his first legit status, where he can feel like a success without worrying that a teacher, or some cop, or some rich kid calling him names, is looking to ruin the moment.

Phipps's strictness helps. For a while, Boogie goes regularly to class. The grades improve. He's not what you'd call a serious student, but he knows a few classmates who are, and he enlists their assistance in the usual way. He can copy their homework, and if he sits close enough, he can copy their test papers. When that fails, he writes answers on his arms and hopes they match up with the right questions.

"Most of the time," he says years later, "I'd write the answers on my arms, and I'd still get six out of ten wrong."

"Truth is, he wasn't a bad kid," Phipps remembers. "Yeah, he sold the football pools, but half the country was doing that. He was a street kid. He had no money. He was in trouble a lot, but it was nothing they'd put him in prison over, no drugs, none of that. He was a rascal. And he needed a chance."

Boogie helps bring some life to City's basketball team, which needed it. With him, they've got a first class backcourt. The other guard is Lee Cornish, whose rainbow jump shots hit from any distance. He and Boogie complement each other. But there's not much talent beyond these two, and so the team's record is so-so. At mid-season, there's doubt they can win bragging rights in the game with big rival Poly.

But the great Boogie experiment's going pretty well. On game days, the bleachers in the school's beat-up old gymnasium are packed. Up there on the little balcony outside the coach's dressing room, there's Phipps' wife, beaming proudly. Standing nearby, a bunch of teachers have come to watch.

Among them is massive George Young. He teaches history and coaches City's varsity football team. He's on his way to bigger places. He'll become a coach with the Baltimore Colts, and the Miami Dolphins, and then he's general manager of the New York Giants and guides them to a Super Bowl triumph. At City, Young's known as a tough cookie with a baleful stare and hulking figure to chill any wayward kid's misbehavior.

But let's take note, at this point, that Boogie's not the only Weinglass brother with athletic connections. Brother Jackie, six years older, had a terrific baseball career when he went to Forest Park High School. A powerful slugger, there were scouts who compared him to another Baltimore ballplayer of his era, Al Kaline.

Kaline played for Southern High and led all prep hitters in batting average. At the same time, Jackie Weinglass was slugging home runs. Kaline went straight from high school to the Detroit Tigers, and then to baseball's Hall of Fame.

Jackie Weinglass got a tryout with the Baltimore Orioles. With manager Paul Richards and a couple of coaches watching, he took batting practice at Memorial Stadium. The pitcher was left-handed. So was Jackie. The pitcher threw big league curve balls. Jackie had never faced a lefty in his whole schoolboy career. On this day, with curve balls fading from his reach, he barely got his bat on the ball. And that was the end of all dreams of a major league career.

But he never quit playing ball. After high school, Jackie hooked on with Hyatt's Men's Clothing. They had stores all around the Baltimore metro area. They specialized in high-end European style merchandise. Jackie worked as a salesman in their Mondawmin Shopping Mall store.

"Nice guy, good salesman," remembered one of the chain's owners, Harvey Hyatt. "But he was still playing in some softball league, and he'd come to work wearing his softball uniform and cleats. This is how he's selling three-piece suits. Nice guy, though."

"Basketball, too," said younger brother Eddie Hyatt. "He'd be selling for us in his basketball shorts."

Then there's Eggy, the middle Weinglass brother, who has his own athletic connections. He runs football pools. These are little cards with point spreads on them, suitable for gambling, familiar in any American city.

Eggy's connected to a bookmaker known as Billy the Kid, who works off The Block, Baltimore's neon area of clubs featuring such quality entertainers as Blaze Starr, Tempest Storm and Irma the Body. They entertain by undressing. The Block is also a hub of numbers runners and sports gamblers.

This is where Billy the Kid comes in. He prints the pools and gets people like Eggy Weinglass to distribute them. The more cards Eggy distributes, the more bets he collects, and the more Eggy's commissions go up from Billy the Kid.

Naturally, being a family guy, Eggy has great interest in his little brother Boogie's academic pursuits. He takes note, for example, that Boogie's newest high school, City College, has about 3,000 students.

"And every one," Eggy explains, "is a potential customer."

It takes no convincing at all to get Boogie into the business. In his entire time at City College, few will see Boogie carrying either notebook or textbook. But many will notice he carries a daily newspaper. He is no student of current events. The newspaper merely hides the cards which list the football point spreads.

Every week, untold numbers of young men at City College, each believing himself quite an expert on matters pertaining to athletics, immerse themselves in these cards and spend their money hoping to score big. They rarely win, but no matter. The betting becomes a rite of passage. This is their little conspiratorial gesture that they're stepping beyond the bounds of grown-ups' suffocating control.

Every week, you can see Boogie out by the stone wall on the side of City separating the main building from the school's mechanical shops. He's there booking his last-minute bets.

"Everybody knew, on Fridays, I'm out at that spot," he remembers. "Guys are lined up."

One time, the action's so heavy that Boogie runs into a slight conflict of interest. It's game day for the varsity basketball team. All other players are down in the gym, in uniform, doing their pre-game warm-ups. The crowd's there, too. Boogie's in uniform, all right, but he's so busy taking bets that he loses track of time and fails to notice the hulking presence suddenly looming behind him.

It's George Young, the 300-pound football coach, who has no patience for this sort of misbehavior. He grabs Boogie around the shoulders and lifts him not quite to eye level.

"What do you think you're doing?" Young says.

"Just trying to make a living," Boogie replies.

Not like this, not while George Young walks the earth. As schoolboy bettors scramble to get away before Young can identify them as co-conspirators, the coach marches Boogie straight down to the gym, where the big crowd is roaring in the last moments before opening tip-off.

Phipps, looking around anxiously for his star guard, finally sees Boogie approaching, inexplicably accompanied by the big football coach.

"I just caught your young man here," Young tells Phipps. "He was booking football bets."

Young doesn't want him playing basketball, he wants him taken out and shot.

"Leonard," says Phipps, going for the full adult measure of authority as Young looks on. Phipps shakes his head. "Leonard," he says, "get out on the court."

Young can't believe what he's hearing.

"You're putting him in the game?" he says.

"Hey," Phipps says, "we're playing Poly."

Decades later, a brief account of that game can be found in the 1961 Greenbag, the City College yearbook. City beats Poly, 70 to 57, it says. Lenny Weinglass scores 28.

Across those winter months, Boogie made his mark and stayed out of visible trouble. He does pretty nicely. At year's end, he's named to the City College Sports Hall of Fame.

But basketball ended too soon. At 19, under Baltimore scholastic rules, he's now too old to play ball. And he's still got a couple of years of schooling ahead of him if he wants to graduate.

He wants to. At 19, he's old enough now to quit. But you drop out of school, you lose serious status. Nettie didn't make her way out of Europe so that her children should walk away from an education. The older Weinglass boys, no great scholars themselves, still managed to get their diplomas. Boogie's friends, many of them now in college, would forever mark him as a loser if he dropped out of high school.

So he stays in school, but with newly flexible boundaries. No longer concerned about basketball eligibility, he's cutting class again. He'll slip down to a little lunch place near school, called Larry's, run by a lady who makes marvelous tuna and tomato sandwiches. Boogie's down there playing cards and shooting the breeze with other scholars who should be in class.

One afternoon, for reasons long since forgotten, he finds himself on a street car somewhere—could be North Avenue, could be Belair Road—somewhere near the center of town. This is the closing era of the city of Baltimore's old trolley cars.

Boogie's got a seat up front. When the conductor stops to let off some passengers, he hears a call for help from the back door. Some elderly person, maybe incapacitated, needs help getting off. The conductor puts the street car in neutral and strides to the back. As he does, Boogie finds inspiration.

"I don't know why," he says all these years later. "I guess I wanted to be funny. It was sick, but I figured it was a smile."

He sits himself down in the conductor's seat. He looks down and sees a huge gas pedal and some gears for shifting. They look just like the gears on an ordinary car—no different, in fact, from a certain police car he once pilfered.

So he shifts gears, and he hijacks the street car. There they are, zipping along the rails, cars everywhere, the conductor calling out to stop as he races on foot trying to catch up, and passengers hollering as though they're being hijacked to Cuba.

"I only went a couple of blocks," Boogie remembers. "Then I got off and ran like hell. You know, it was bad enough I stole a police car."

Sometimes he gets caught, and sometimes not. At City College, he's getting sent down to principal Henry Yost's office on what feels like a daily basis. He's there often enough that the old man gets pretty accustomed to Boogie being in the room, like a relative.

One day, thinking nothing of it, Yost wanders out of his office. He leaves Boogie sitting there by himself. This is a fundamental mistake. There, in what he imagined was a safe storage place, Yost has neglected to close the door. Boogie spies the contents inside.

"Blank report cards," he says. "It was a no-brainer."

He takes all of them, maybe 200 altogether. When word slowly filters through the various classrooms at City, many consider this a godsend. Buy a blank report card, fill in any grades you like, and impress your parents how hard you've worked and how much you deserve the family car on weekends.

He charges five bucks apiece for the report cards, or sometimes ten. It's pretty good money back then, most of which Boogie happily brings home to his mother. He knows how she struggles.

Nobody at City knows where these report cards came from, but everybody knows Boogie Weinglass is the guy to go to. It adds to the legend. Some say he broke into school headquarters, down on 25th Street, to filch them. Yeah, they whisper, that sounds like something Boogie would do. This, from guys who have never actually laid eyes on him but have heard some of the stories.

Like the one about the cherry bomb. As the tale goes, Boogie's sitting in class one day but not getting a lot out of it. He's sitting in the back of the room, next to a door. The teacher's got his back turned. And Boogie tosses this cherry bomb against the front blackboard, where it goes off like a grenade.

Boogie bolts out the back door and spends the rest of the hour happily goofing off somewhere—only to return, at the end of class, pretending to be out of breath as he approaches the teacher.

"Weinglass, where have you been?" the teacher asks.

"I chased that sucker as far as I could," he says, "but I couldn't catch him."

Decades later, Boogie can't recall the fake chase, but he admits the part about the cherry bomb is absolutely true.

"History class," he says. "Teacher's writing on the blackboard, so he's got his back to us. I lit it right there in class. Couple of guys see me, but they don't say nothing. And I threw it up to the front, like a bowling ball.

"It stops right at the teacher's heel. It goes off, loud as could be. He practically had a heart attack. He turns around and says one word: 'Weinglass.' Knew it was me right away. Threw me out of class."

What about the other story—"Chased that guy as far as I could." No truth to that?

"Don't remember," Boogie shrugs. "Could have been another time, another cherry bomb."

By some miracle out of scripture, Boogie survives all of this—almost. It's the autumn of his senior year, and he's scheduled to graduate just after Christmas break. He's in one of the public school system's last mid-year graduating classes. Twenty years old, he's so close to graduation, and so much older than so many of these pimply kids all around him, that by now he's frantic to get his diploma.

But then somebody tells Henry Yost about the football pools. And Yost, the kindest of men, hits the roof. It's not just that one of his City lads is breaking the law. Hell, City's filled with all kinds of kids, some of them not exactly choirboys. But Yost feels betrayed. He's let this kid off the hook so many times, and now he's been blind-sided.

He calls Boogie into his office once again, and this time he lays down the law.

"You're suspended," he says, "and you can't come back until you bring your mother with you."

"My mother?"

"That's right, young man. Your mother."

This is a game changer. This will break Nettie's heart if she learns the full extent of her youngest son's outrages. What's more, she'll tell Yankel, and Jackie will come after Boogie and throw him into another wall.

"I didn't have a choice," Boogie reflects 60 years later. "My life was on the line."

And so, seeing no other options, he brings to the halls of City College a woman not precisely his mother, but someone posing as Nettie.

He brings Kank.

"To do what?" she asks when Boogie makes his request.

"To get me back in school," Boogie explains. "Kanky, I can't come back without bringing my mother. Yost don't know what my mother looks like. Kanky, I want to graduate. I'm 20 years old, and I'm right on the edge."

Kank finds this pretty touching. The boys who come to her house are always looking for one thing only, and mothering ain't it. Boogie's been there even when he's not looking for action. So she agrees to go along with the con.

And so, one fine morning, we find the two of them, Boogie and Kank, sitting down in Henry Yost's office, hearing the worst of the Weinglass history.

Yost is a gentle man with a raspy voice normally so soft that it's tough to hear him. But he's doing his best to show the alleged Mrs. Weinglass that he's had it with her wayward son.

"He cuts school all the time, Mrs. Weinglass," says Yost.

"He's been sick a lot," says Kank.

"He gets into fights."

"Only when provoked."

"Mrs. Weinglass," says Yost, holding up the thick folder he's kept on Boogie, "just look at this."

Now Kank's feeling pretty bad. Boogie's depending on her to get him through this crisis, and she feels she's letting him down.

"Leonard," says Yost, "is just no good."

No good?

"Now, wait a minute," Kank cries. She's halfway out of her chair now. She goes after Yost, calling him names, attacking the entire school system of the city of Baltimore.

"You can't talk that way about my son," she hollers.

She goes on like this, and Yost sits there stunned. In this moment, she's not Kank, the easy sexual mark of half the high school boys of northwest Baltimore. She's Kank the Defender, Kank the Aggrieved Mother.

"She definitely over-reacted," Boogie recalls years later. "I thought she was gonna take a swing at Yost." But she's so convincing, the kindly principal says he'll give Boogie one more chance.

So he hangs in there. He isn't kicked out, and he doesn't drop out. He's still getting into fights whenever some idiot frat boy calls him a dirtball, or some drape makes a Jew remark, but he's doing his best to stay out of trouble.

And he's feeling the stirrings of something previously unfelt. Call it love, call it maturity, his feelings for his newest girlfriend, Joanie Sutton, go beyond anything he's felt before. She's a cheerleader at Milford Mill High School, out in northwest Baltimore County. In the closing months of high school, she's his steady, in spite of her parents.

They warn her about him. The father runs a successful auto parts business down on North Avenue. The mother dotes on daughter Joanie and two sons, both of whom work down at the family firm. The parents look at Boogie and issue major warnings.

"My parents, my God, what they said about him," Joanie recalls years later. "My mother said, 'I raised you to be a hothouse flower, and you're running with the weeds.' This was not what they had in mind for me.

"But this was part of the excitement. I was a straight-laced kid and he was this wild and crazy bad boy. Did he get into fights all the time? Absolutely. Did he threaten people when we went out? Absolutely. Did he scare people? Absolutely. Did we have fights? I don't remember. But that doesn't mean they didn't happen.

"But he wasn't an angry kid, he was a sweet kid. Why was he wild? It's how he got noticed. He was great at basketball, and he could run and do goofy things and get attention. I think it was the need for attention."

Or, as she told GQ Magazine, in a lengthy feature the magazine ran on Boogie in 1990, "It's like a kid who's dyslexic, so he throws books. If Boogie couldn't afford the navy blazers and the Weejuns, then he was going to be the opposite. He wasn't going to care about any of that and would excel in other things, like fighting and being wild and crazy."

Now, 30 years since that national magazine reflection, she recalls the Weinglass family dysfunction and adds, "His mother was attentive, but she was left with these three crazy boys. His father was a very sweet, sickly man, but he gambled everything away. His mother would say to me, 'Don't you let my son gamble.' She was about four-feet-ten, and she was nervous, hysterical, always yelling because nobody paid attention to her. And my parents are telling me, 'You want to be part of this?'"

By this time, Joanie's 17 years old and ready to graduate high school. She's talking about going away to college. Boogie's 20 and desperate to graduate from City. The thought of going to college does not precisely cross his mind.

He still hangs out at the diner, and at Benny's and Knocko's. But he can't help noticing that the old crowd's thinned out. Many of his pals have moved on. They're in college now, or they're working for a living. Some of them only come home for holidays. That feeling of being left behind—on Baker Street, where so many families moved away, and then on Violet Avenue where the same thing's been happening—he can feel it all over again as the months pass since his 20th birthday and he's still a high school guy.

In his fashion, he's done his best. He swallowed his pride. He listened to his mother, and he listened to Jackie, and he didn't drop out. And now he comes down to his final days of high school, and all he needs is passing grades to graduate.

But he falls short. He's got his final report card in his hands, and he's made it through every class but one. It's chemistry. Mr. Schwartz's chemistry class. As everybody at City knows, Schwartz is an old-school tough guy who not only teaches chemistry but prowls the hallways eyeballing any student who attempts to go to his locker when it's not a specifically assigned time for this.

One day, he catches a sophomore breaking the locker rules, and Schwartz tells him he's got to stay after school for this offense. "Report to my room at the close of school," he says.

The culprit is Allan Charles, the kid who turned to Boogie a while back for help with some of those drapes giving him a rough time. Charles is sitting in Schwartz's front row now, doing after-school punishment work, writing, "I must not go to my locker during class time" a hundred times. And into the room walks Boogie.

Schwartz is standing there with a test tube in his hands and a slide rule in his short-sleeve white shirt pocket. Boogie walks in with his report card in his hand. His voice is somewhere between despair and disbelief, between barely controlled anger and naked desperation.

"I'm 20 fuckin' years old," he tells Schwartz, "and I'm a senior in high school."

He hands Schwartz his report card with the failing chemistry grade.

"You just failed me, and I am 20 years old, and I can't graduate from fucking high school."

"That's because you're a moron," Schwartz tells him.

Charles is sitting there and can't believe the confrontation playing out in front of him.

"I gotta get the fuck out of here," Boogie says now. "I'm 20 years old, and I gotta graduate. You're the only thing between me and graduation."

Schwartz says nothing. He's not about to budge, not for this kid who hasn't even paid attention all year.

"If you don't pass me," says Boogie, "I'm gonna kick the living shit out of you and everybody in your whole fuckin' family."

At which point, the words have definitely punctured the consciousness of old-school tough guy Schwartz, who looks at him and forthrightly declares:

"Let me see what I can do."

And this is how Leonard Michael Weinglass, aka Boogie, became a graduate of the public schools of the city of Baltimore.

Chapter Seven

The Graduate

Now that the public schools of Baltimore have failed to tame him, a few more powerful institutions will attempt to corral the various Weinglass impulses: the Maryland National Guard (not likely) and marriage (even unlikelier.)

He joins the National Guard after high school graduation, since he's got no immediate job prospects, and Joanie's got another six months of high school. So why not sign up, avoid the threat of getting drafted and serving in some godforsaken outlet like Korea, the way his brother Eggy did?

Boogie's time in uniform is barely tolerated, though he's stationed at Fort Knox, near America's money. He's not crazy about being awakened at dawn. He vows, when this is over, he'll find some job where he never has to awaken before 11. This vow, unlike others, he will honor.

He's not too crazy about these five-mile runs, carrying full packs of equipment, that his entire platoon faces. Fortunately, he finds ways to avoid them. Back in Baltimore, Joanie's phone will ring, and it's Boogie on the line.

"Where are you?" she asks.

"Hiding," he explains.

Almost as bad as these full-pack jaunts and these early morning wake-up calls, he arrives just in time for a rare snow-filled Kentucky winter. Then, go figure, he consistently ticks off his drill sergeant.

"Weinglass, drop and gimme 20," he hears a lot.

"Push-ups in the snow," says Boogie, still feeling the chill. "You never saw a guy do them faster."

That's not the biggest problem. He always had a thick, wavy head of hair, but now they've shaved it all off. When they did this to brother Eggy, it revealed the egg shape of his head, thus giving him an unfortunate nickname to carry for the rest of his life. Boogie's a little self-conscious about his own haircut, thinking it makes his nose look bigger. He's standing in chow line one day, not long after he gets there, when he's shoved from behind.

"Some big hillbilly from West Virginia, a lot bigger than me," he says. "Tells me, 'Move on, Jewboy.' I hit him right in the fuckin' face. I caught him perfectly. We're rolling around, I'm on top, and this sergeant pulled me off. He picked me up with one hand. And he wasn't fuckin' around.

"He says, 'You like to fight? I'll tell you where you're gonna fight. This Friday, in front of the whole platoon.' That was the entertainment. I'm now fighting with this guy Wall, in front of everybody. And they're all rooting for me, 'cause he's a hell of a lot bigger than me. And I beat the shit out of him. They stopped the fight in the third round."

This was his first boxing match, and not his last. He becomes a Friday night regular, undefeated, though a few fights he describes as close ones. "I bled easy from my big nose," he says. When he's not boxing, they've got him working as a medical orderly in the camp hospital, everything from changing sheets to picking up bodies and moving them to the morgue.

In his quiet hours, he notices he misses Joanie. This is new territory of the heart for him, which he converts to his usual impulsiveness. When his basic training's done in early summer, and he gets back to Baltimore, he sits down for a serious talk about where he and Joanie are going with the rest of their lives. This, from a guy who never plans 14 seconds into the future, and a girl who's never been away from home.

"I was supposed to go off to the University of Miami," Joanie remembers, "but I was scared of going. I'd never been away. I'd never even been to sleep-away camp."

Boogie, against all odds, had late-arriving thoughts of going to college. He'd gotten more than a dozen offers of basketball scholarships. Small schools, like the old Western Maryland College, in Westminster, each of them willing to overlook his academic records because some scout had watched him play ball. He enrolled at the University of Baltimore, which accepted all warm bodies in that era, but dropped out after a few months.

"I was gung ho," he remembers, "but I had no money. I had to go make some. I was too poor for too long. And I knew my basketball limitations. I knew I wasn't going pro, or even Division I college ball. And Joanie was going away, and I was gonna stay behind in Baltimore."

"We were sitting in my car," Joanie remembers, "and Boogie says, 'You're gonna go off to school and meet somebody, and we're never gonna see each other again. We gotta get married.' I'm already scared of going away, so this sounds good. So I go home and tell my parents about this."

Hysteria ensues. First it's the parents, then Joanie. The mother's ready to collapse, the father's ready to commit murder. So Joanie responds accordingly.

"If you don't let me marry him, and give me a big wedding," she tells her folks, "I'll run away and you'll never see me get married."

The father, a reasonable man, offers compromise. He wants a sit-down with Boogie, figuring he'll talk the young man out of all this craziness.

"Her father," says Boogie, "wanted to kill me."

They meet in the Sutton home. As the two men sit at a small kitchen table, Joanie and her mother exit to another room.

Boogie begins, "Sir, I'd like permission…" when a powerful hand wraps itself around his skinny wrist. Don't say another word. Joanie's father's not a tall man, but he's solid as an industrial fire hydrant, and now he's squeezing Boogie's wrist so hard, he's cutting off all flow of blood.

"If you ever lay a hand on my daughter," he says. The look of sheer menace on his face finishes the threat for him.

The old man's done a little research. He has friends in the police department with access to the full Weinglass folder: the time or two he swiped police cars, the hot-wiring of that teacher's car at Forest Park, the football pools, the fighting, everything but the blank report cards.

"You don't want your daughter with him," the police say.

As he recites these police reports, Joanie's father hasn't released his grip on Boogie's wrist. By the time he's finished, all the blood is gone from the Weinglass arm.

"He'd have beaten me in a fight," says Boogie. "I remember the strength. And he wasn't letting go."

Then Joanie's mother comes back to the kitchen. She has the sense that things aren't going well, and she's been getting a mouthful from her daughter, who's still threatening to revolt.

"Jack, leave him alone," she tells her husband. Reluctantly, he lets go of Boogie's wrist. The mother says, "I'm sorry, Leonard."

Never mind any of those police reports, never mind all warnings, nor all parental instinct to protect their daughter. And never mind what the former Joanie Weinglass says, 60 years later, in retrospect.

"We were children. I have no idea what we were thinking."

In the coming days, Boogie turned to a pal, Larry Oberfeld, who had understanding parents. The father had a bar, and the mother was touched by tales of romance. When informed Boogie wanted to get married, they scrounged up $200 to help him buy a proper engagement ring.

The wedding's a blast—a big affair at Emerald Gardens, just as Joanie wanted it—and then Boogie went to work at the family business, Standard Auto Parts, down on North Avenue. The job's not bad, the money's steady, and Boogie's learning how to deal with customers by watching Joanie's brothers. But he's spending too many nights making too many long-shot bets that don't come in. He's still running the football pools on the side. And he's still, at heart, a street kid.

"His boyfriends were always more important than I was, always," Joanie recalls. "It was important to be popular on the playground. That was, like, his thing in life, and I didn't get it."

She's adapting to Boogie's family, as well.

"His mother was about four-feet-ten, and she was attentive, but she had these three crazy sons," Joanie remembers, "and so she was nervous, hysterical, always yelling because nobody paid attention to her. She'd tell me, 'Don't you let him gamble.' Like I had a choice.

"His brothers were very welcoming to me. My parents bought me a car. Jackie wanted to give me his car. He'd wash it once a week or more. He wanted to give it to us. When Boogie was in basic training, Eggy bought me a poodle to keep me company. Both of them looked out for Boogie. But then the roles reversed as the years went on. Boogie was the brighter one, and the more successful. He looked out for them."

While the marriage is still alive, Joanie's working as a hair dresser and making pretty decent money. She says Boogie should stop working for her daddy and take a shot at this. So he starts going to hair dressing school, the Star Beauty Academy, Reisterstown Road and Rogers Avenue, familiar territory. It's around the corner from the Hilltop Diner and across the street from the Hilltop Bowling Alley where brother Eggy now hangs out every day and runs his football pools. At the "academy," he's not called Boogie, he's known as Mister Lenny, for a little class.

The Star Beauty Academy "was 28 girls," says Boogie, "and one flashy gay guy wearing makeup and lipstick, and macho Boogie. It got me in my share of fights when guys heard about it. Fraternity boys calling me a fag and a sissy. I can't tell you how many guys I had to beat up because of that."

But there's a bigger problem. The gambling's getting worse, and the losing's getting bigger. He told Joanie he wouldn't gamble. But now he owes a local bookmaker $5,000, such big money in the early '60 that a frantic Boogie had to beg help from Joanie's brothers, Frank and Billy. Either pay off the bookie, or the guy's threatening to hurt Joanie.

"Always some kind of gambling," Joanie recalls. "I remember a Saturday night when we were supposed to go out somewhere. He said he was too tired and needed to go to sleep. Next thing I know, he slipped out in the middle of the night to play cards. My father was home every night with my mother. I thought that's the way married people behaved."

A year and a half into the marriage, she says, "I decided I'm not having a good time, and I'm leaving in the morning. And that was it. I was 18 and not feeling loved or cared about."

But, from a distance of nearly 60 years, Joanie says, "I'll say this for Boogie. He told somebody, 'Joanie was just a little girl. All she wanted was to be loved, and I didn't know how.' That's why I still love him. And, if he needed me, I'd run to him today. And I know he'd do the same if I needed anything."

Now, no longer married and no longer working in the family firm or the beauty business, Boogie needed a job and a place to live. And who comes out of the blue but old rent-collecting pal Harold Goldsmith. He's got a spare bedroom in an apartment.

It's not a bad place, and they can split the rent. An odd coupling, of course, but they're each grateful for a familiar face in a transitional moment in their young lives.

And then Boogie gets into more trouble. There's a fight at the Hilltop Diner. "Some hillbilly makes a Jew remark," he says, "and I knocked out a few of his teeth and then fled the scene."

He's back at the apartment, with Harold, when there's knocking on the door. Boogie's in the bathroom shaving and doesn't hear it when the cops come barging in. They're frisking Harold, who's definitely not accustomed to this kind of chaos in his life. The cops say they're looking for Boogie.

"Boog, come out here," Harold calls out. "The police want to see you."

Boogie's got shaving cream all over his face, and he's not wearing a shirt.

"Tell 'em I'm shaving," he calls back.

That buys him a few seconds. While the cops are still at the front door, giving Harold a hard time, Boogie runs into the nearest bedroom. He climbs atop a dresser, which is next to a window. He tips open a screen, looks down, sees it's not too far to the grass below. And he jumps.

No shirt, half-shaven, and he runs. He runs like it's the old races up Reisterstown Road at 2 in the morning, except now at least he's wearing pants. When he finds a pay phone several blocks away, he calls Harold back at the apartment.

"Boog, the police are really angry," Harold says. "You gotta get back here."

"I don't think so, Harold."

"Gimme the phone," one of the officers tells Harold.

The cop affects a calm demeanor when he greets Boogie.

"Where are you?" he inquires.

"That's your job to find out," Boogie replies. "You have no right to break in."

"Well, come back and let's talk about it."

"I don't think so. And, by the way, Harold had nothing to do with this."

"No problem, we know that. But you beat somebody up and fled the scene."

"What was I supposed to do, stay there?"

Eventually, the cops left the apartment, and Boogie stayed away for a few days until the cops lost interest. Then, when the case finally reached a district court, a lenient judge gave probation, and what passed for normalcy was restored to Boogie's world.

Now he finds a new job. It's nothing glamorous, but it's steady work in the basement of a downtown clothing warehouse, Highlander Leather and Suede and Glenhaven Suits. Pays $8 an hour, and he has to punch a time clock, but the money's not bad for the mid-'60s.

And it's his first taste of the business of fashion.

When orders come in to the warehouse, it's Boogie's job to pick out the right outfits, put them in a box, and ship them out. He's there a couple of months, on automatic pilot, when he notices a salesman's name on an invoice. And he sees that the salesman gets a commission. All the salesmen get commission money. Suddenly, the biggest dream of Boogie's life is to be a salesman.

This is facilitated, strictly by accident, when he gets himself in trouble for a change. One floor up from the basement, that's where the company's chief financial officer works. And he's got four young ladies also working there.

Boogie's up there a little too often to suit the CFO. He warns Boogie about excessive flirting. Boogie pays no attention, as usual. The CFO's a little full of himself. He's a middle-age guy in a dress-up suit, and Boogie's in jeans and a tee shirt every day. Obviously, he doesn't know his place in the pecking order, and doesn't care that the CFO's getting ticked off.

"You're fired," he tells Boogie.

Instead of skulking out the door in defeat, Boogie takes a last-second desperation shot. He goes up to the second floor, where the company's president, a fellow named Leo Thomas, has his office. The door's open. Boogie stands there, looking in at Thomas, who's behind a big desk in a suit and tie. Boogie's in his usual jeans and tee shirt, full of basement dust.

"Can I help you?"

"Yes, sir. I work downstairs. I'd like to be a salesman."

"Where is it you work?"

"The basement, the warehouse."

"What's your name?"

"Leonard Weinglass."

"Leonard Weinglass?" says the president of the company. "You mean Boogie?"

How do you like this? The legend of Boogie has reached the grown-ups!

"Yes, I'm Boogie."

"What are you doing here? Why aren't you playing college basketball?"

"I have to make a living," Boogie replies.

Turns out, Thomas' nephew was a substitute on City College's basketball team, and he came to see a game. He knew at least one thing about Boogie: this was a young guy full of aggressiveness.

"Can you sell?" Thomas asks.

"Yes, sir."

Thomas picks up the phone and calls somebody in New York, where a fellow named Bernie Gold answers.

"Bernie, I got a kid here who wants to sell." Bernie says something back to Leo that Boogie can't hear. Leo says, "Boogie, when can you get to New York?"

"Tomorrow."

The next day, Boogie's on a Metroliner to New York. He hasn't even got decent dress-up clothes. It's a freezing winter day, and he's borrowed his brother Jackie's overcoat, herringbone with a velvet collar. It's a few sizes too big for him, but at least it makes a nice impression. He wore his best pair of shoes, which are leftovers from his bar mitzvah nearly a decade ago.

"I didn't even know how to get on a train," he remembers.

Nor, it turns out, how to get back on the train once he got off.

On his way to New York, the train gets stuck in Philadelphia. Everything's backed up in a major East coast snowstorm. Boogie's running late for his job interview and fears the opportunity's slipping away. Frantically, as the train sits there in Philly, he asks a conductor where he can find the nearest pay phone.

"Out there," the conductor says, pointing vaguely to the platform. "But you better get back fast, we're leaving in five minutes."

Boogie makes it back in six.

The train's leaving, Boogie's running alongside of it, waving his arms, hollering like crazy, trying to get it to stop. "Hey! Hey! Hey!" The train moves on. There goes the job interview, he figures. Also, not to be minimized, he left Jackie's herringbone coat with the velvet collar on the train, and that's gone, too. Jackie will murder him for this. What should he do about that, hide out at Kank's for another week?

"We have another train coming," somebody in a railroad uniform tells him.

When he finally gets to New York, he walks into a ferocious mix of snow and rain, and he's got no overcoat. He's spitting snow, it's so torrential. His hair's all over the place. His clothes are soaked. His heart's pounding, and he's got a pretty good walk before he reaches his interview—unless it's too late and everybody's gone home already.

And, naturally, he's still thinking: Jackie's going to murder him when he finds out about the overcoat.

When he walks into Bernie Gold's office, he meets a nice man with a smiling face, and all worries slip behind him.

"Relax, kid," says Gold. "We heard nice things about you. Everything's gonna be all right."

Chapter Eight

"My Motivation Was Poverty"

And then he's gone.

Gone from Nettie and Eggy and Jackie, gone from the gang at Benny's and the diner, gone from football pools and street fights, and gone from Baltimore.

For now.

The company gives him two weeks of intensive training in New York, and then they send him south. He's a traveling salesman with a home base in Atlanta and a swath of territory stretching across Georgia and the Carolinas, the eastern part of Alabama and parts of Florida.

Turns out the company's short of talent down there, which is one reason they were so quick to hire him. The timing's perfect, and so is the arrangement. The company gets a hustler, and Boogie gets to pursue dreams of big commissions.

Was he sentimental leaving home? Not really, he says. "I was tired of being poor, and I wanted to make some god-damn money. My motivation was poverty. And I wanted to be a success. They were telling me I could make $40,000 a year. I thought they were exaggerating."

But not for long. When he arrives in Atlanta, the senior salesman there picks him up. He's driving a Cadillac convertible. He's a little guy, maybe five-feet-five, not very imposing. But he's wearing a Rolex watch, and he's got flashy rings on three fingers. And that Cadillac, all by itself, gives Boogie visions of the future.

Two things happen right away. First, he starts making phone calls to the buyers at stores. Second, he gets nowhere at all. There's a whole world of sales people trying to hustle them, and the buyers say they're too busy to see him, or they're "all bought up for the season."

So, forget the phone calls. Boogie goes straight into the stores, dragging along his merchandise on a metal rolling rack, scores of different items, different colors, different sizes, and he's really turning on the charm.

And doing only marginally better.

So he gets another idea. Who wants to drag all this stuff around, anyway, packing samples into his trunk, pulling them out of the trunk, lugging all of it in and out of stores? It's hot down South, hotter than Baltimore! And, anyway, what buyer wants to sift through so many items that they become a blur?

So he downsizes. Forget the advance phone calls, forget the rolling racks. He walks into big department stores now and says, "Where's the buyer's office?" Goes straight to the buyers, bangs on their office doors. Only there's no rolling rack with a hundred different items, there's just Boogie and a handful of his very best stuff, and it's dangling from his arm.

"Is this cool, or what?" he asks.

"Who are you?" the buyers reply.

They get past introductions real fast, because the stuff on his arm is always his most striking merchandise. And he builds from those, and he's no longer some stranger on the phone, he's certain he's now a guy who's going to make money for everybody.

He's been on the job for five weeks when he gets called back to Baltimore. Big meeting of the company's entire national fleet of salesmen. Fellow named Archie Gross is running the meeting, and as Boogie looks around, he sees a bunch of middle aged men, dressed in coats and ties and wearing lots of jewelry, the gaudy symbols they flash to assure themselves they're successful, they really are. The old insecurities start narrowing in on him: Is he in the same league with these grown-ups?

"We've got our most exciting line," Gross is saying now, "and I want to ask a question. I want to know why this kid over there"—he points to Boogie, who's sitting there as unobtrusively as possible—"Leonard, stand up."

Heart pounding. What is it this time, another classroom lecture about another failing grade? What's he done wrong this time? He didn't cheat off anybody's test paper, so what's the problem? So he stands.

"I want to know," Gross says, "why this kid here sold more than the 12 of you"—he's pointing to the front row of salesmen—"put together—put together—in one month, and opened up 20 new accounts, and you guys collectively didn't open that many. I want to know why he's been here five weeks, and he's sold more than anybody in this room."

He's made Boogie Weinglass, the kid who couldn't pass a test without leaning across some brainy classmate's paper, into the smartest guy in the whole company. He's still standing there, all eyes on him, when he hears Gross say, "Tell these fellows how you do it."

So he does. He goes through the whole five-week history of what he's learned, right down to his opening moment with each buyer, where he holds up his handful of top items.

"Before I even introduce myself," he tells these veterans, "I hold up the merchandise. They don't care what your name is. They care about the goods."

So he's a hit. He settles into an apartment in Atlanta, and he gets the lay of the land. He joins the local Jewish Community Center so he can play basketball, and he makes his mark there because he's varsity material against a bunch of playground types.

And he discovers the local night spots such as the Playboy Club and a joint called The Scene, where strobe lights are blinking and half the airline stewardesses in America seem to be in town every night. Nobody in Atlanta's seen dance moves like this out of a white boy before this. True to his army vow, the life-style means he gets in late, and sleeps until he's fully rested.

Atlanta's getting pretty hip around this time. Across much of the south in the '60s, racial tension covers everything like a funeral shroud. In some cities, they're turning vicious dogs on black people who dare to ask for the right to vote. They're turning fire hoses on blacks who want to go to "public" schools always reserved for white children. Before the decade's over, some bigot with a rifle will cut down Dr. Martin Luther King and set loose fire and rage in scores of American cities.

But Atlanta's a slightly different story. It's so hip—especially by southern standards—that some people are calling it the San Francisco of the South. Scarlett O'Hara might have lived here—in fiction, anyway—but she's not only buried now but so is her ghost.

The city's got a sizeable counter culture. Part college student and part disenchanted street kids, they've found their voice in a weekly paper called The Great Speckled Bird, which is hustled on the street and dares to take on the city's ruling elite even when the daily papers are too timid.

There's a thriving night counter-culture as well: young people, musicians, people who want to stay out late and have a good time. It takes Boogie about ten minutes to discover this world and make it his own.

"I'm out clubbing all the time," he remembers. "Atlanta was pretty unbelievable back then. I remember a place called The Scene. Lights blinking and great music and people dancing, which I loved. And beautiful women."

Atlanta's also drawing national corporations. They're setting up regional headquarters in the town, and filling offices with smart young professionals. These newcomers are making good money, and they're spending it like crazy.

Some of these people are black. Atlanta's got one of the most affluent black populations in the country, and they're starting to flex their muscles in politics and business and spreading new money around.

When Boogie's not busy discovering all the pleasures of his new home base, he's on the road selling clothes, opening new accounts, and making what he considers an interesting discovery: the stores across the south don't have very hip taste. And one thing about this guy, he's been a student of style his whole life. He's been watching what the other kids were wearing, sometimes enviously, sometimes disdainfully, while he was wearing his brothers' hand-me-downs.

But it's more than a sense of style, it's a feel for what's going on in the culture itself. And, here in the late '60s, with the war in Vietnam building up, and assassinations and riots tearing the country apart, there's a whole revolution in clothing—especially young people's clothing—that reflects the rebellious, unsettling times. And he sees none of this reflected in these stores across the South.

That instinct deepens when he makes trips up to New York. The company sends him there for another meeting of sales reps. He's got a day or two to walk around while he's there, so he decides to wander a little.

It's that little pocket of time between the exit of the beatniks and the entrance of the hippies. Underground poetry's morphing into rebellious music, and the street fashions implicitly reject anything that smacks of capitulation to adulthood, of the dreary, controlling, overbearing workday world.

He's walking past a Manhattan store called Different Drummer and notices a sign they've posted in the window: "Tired of the Same Old Shit? Come On In." Are they kidding? Who uses language like that to sell clothes? So he walks into the place. The encounter will teach him lessons in fashion, and in marketing.

Two sales women—"New York knockouts," he says—come up to him. He's wearing dress pants, dress shoes, and a white shirt. They ask him how old he is. They can't believe he's in his 20s and dressed like such a straight-ass.

"We've got to get you out of that shirt and pants and into some jeans," one of them says. Minutes later he comes out of a dressing room in a pair of tight jeans and a tee shirt with a smiley logo that fits tight around his arms. They tell him he looks good. He asks each of them out on a date. Sorry, they've each got boyfriends.

"But I went down swinging," he says later.

When he looks in a mirror, he likes what he sees. The outfit's anti-preppy, it's not some button-down shirt and khakis like the snotty high school fraternity boys used to wear. It's funky, it's a little outlandish. He decides, in that specific instant, that this is the future.

So now he's not just a salesman hustling his company's merchandise, he's a dreamer mulling fashion ideas. When he hits these stores across the south, he continues to be unimpressed with the stuff they're carrying. It's yesterday's notion of fashion. It's tired, it's as though the '60s haven't arrived yet.

He's also getting ticked off with his company—specifically, with the senior sales guy down here, the fellow who picked him up that first day in the Cadillac convertible. The guy's squeezing him on commissions. Boogie's making all these new customers, but his pay checks aren't reflecting the kind of money he ought to be taking home.

He makes friends with a fellow named Bob Levy, who's assistant manager in a warehouse specializing in bathroom products. They meet at an Atlanta night spot and realize they're both single guys looking for a roommate. They move in together the next day, and then Boogie helps Levy find a job as a lingerie salesman. He's selling bras and girdles, and he's got the same territory as Boogie. So they're roommates, and they're on the road together, too, for the next two years.

"A great time of our lives," Levy remembers. Fifty years later, he's still living down in the Atlanta area, each day "another great day in paradise," he calls it. But those years with Weinglass he recalls with special affection.

"You might call me Boogie's wing man," he says, laughing aloud. "We'd go into a town, and we shared a lot of clients." Levy's doing girdles and bras, and Boogie's doing women's outerwear.

"And he's hitting on every pretty girl he sees," Levy says. "If one of us scored, we'd stay overnight in that town. He had one of the great pickup lines. It's April, or it's July, it doesn't matter.

He goes up to some girl and says, "What are you doing New Year's Eve?'"

It's like saying, Can I take you to the high school prom? You can call me later and say you can't make it, but for right now, let's think long-range. Not this Friday or next Tuesday, but something special. New Year's. Or prom night. That's how much I think of you.

"That was my open," Boogie remembers. "Or, 'Excuse me, have you always been this pretty?' That always gets their attention. Or, if I saw a guy talking to a girl and I couldn't butt in, I'd wait until he walked away, and I'd say, 'I hate to tell you, but the guy you're talking to is gay.' I did everything under the sun."

Today such language is considered politically incorrect; back then, it was considered close maneuvering in the erogenous zone, and a smile. The guys might say something inappropriate, but the girls were free to say, "Get lost."

"Boogie was absolutely fearless," Levy says. "If I was up against him, hitting on a chick, I always lost, a hundred percent. He was the master. And we got along great. On the road, or in the apartment. He liked to sleep late and go to bed late. I was the opposite. And we're both chasing after every pretty girl in town. Everywhere we went in Atlanta, everybody knew him, all the clubs, all the top chicks in town who adored him. He's the most incredible person I've met in my life."

Fearless, too, on the job. He was bringing in big business for Highlander Leather and Suede, but seething over the size of his pay checks. He and Levy start talking about opening their own business.

Levy's still with the lingerie company, which sends him up to New York for a sales meeting. The woman who's the designer of the company's line takes Levy down to Greenwich Village to walk around. He mentions to her that all the other salesmen are middle aged guys still dressing like it's the Eisenhower years.

She agrees. She starts putting an outfit together for Levy: Nehru jacket, bell bottom pants, platform shoes. When he shows up at the next day's meeting, the salesmen laugh at him. But the women love the new outfit.

"And I noticed," Levy remembers, "when we were down in the Village, in this boutique down there, all these women were braless, and they wore tank tops or tubes, and they had on bell bottoms. It was like, holy shit, this is what I want to do, have a place like this."

When he gets back to Atlanta, he tells this to Boogie, who identifies immediately. He tells Levy he's been selling bell bottoms from the trunk of his car, and people love them. And, on TV one night, he saw Sammy Davis Jr.

"He was wearing a pair of black tight pants that fit snug around his thighs and then flared out into bell bottoms," he recalled half a century later. "And that's the start of me making a fortune on bell bottoms."

"Why are we busting our asses for somebody else," Levy asks one day, "when we could open our own place?"

He doesn't need to sell Boogie, who's angry over his belief that he's getting cheated on commissions. Now they're swapping fashion ideas, they're looking at real estate locations.

They're laying the foundation for a billion-dollar empire and a revolution in fashion.

Chapter Nine

"Don't Phuque with the Pants"

In the turbulent 1960s, no year was more convulsive than 1968, when America seemed at war with itself. That's the year the first Merry-Go-Round opened on the scruffy section of Atlanta's Peachtree Street that would become known as The Strip. The store became a smile in the heart of municipal grief.

This was the year the assassination of Dr. Martin Luther King set off riots in almost every big American city, but not Atlanta. This was King's home town. The killing, and the violent aftermath, came in Memphis, in April. Merry-Go-Round opened that July.

Across America that spring, riots devastated more than a hundred cities. Thousands were injured, tens of thousands arrested, and large swaths of urban areas burned to the ground. A veil of ash seemed to cover the whole country.

In Atlanta, 200,000 people followed a mule-drawn wagon to King's funeral and sang "We Shall Overcome." This honored King's message of non-violence. In most cities, though, the fires burned across days and seemed to symbolize some irretrievable break with the past.

Here was a literal passing of the torch to a new generation, black and white, enflamed not only by American racism but by cynical politics, by endless war in Vietnam, and by unchanging economic and cultural divides. It felt like a revolution. Now young people needed to clothe themselves for it.

Weinglass and Levy thought they were opening a funky little boutique and instead caught a cultural wave and started an empire. They found a beat-up, abandoned grocery store on a block that had seen better days.

The place was a mess. "The landlord was thrilled just to get somebody in there," Bob Levy remembered. "I think it had been empty for several years. It still had a freezer sitting in the middle of the place, which we couldn't get out of there. We used it as part of our display. We put a chair on top of it and put a pretty girl up there to watch for shoplifters. She couldn't have caught one if they'd stood up and declared they were shoplifting, but it became a fixture."

Before Merry-Go-Round's arrival, the 1000 block of Peachtree Street was a forlorn stretch of urban waste less than a mile from high-end downtown Atlanta. Half a dozen abandoned store fronts punctuated the desolation. Some buildings on the block had been set afire - not for political statement but for insurance profit - and their remains turned into parking lots.

Weinglass and Levy moved into 1007 Peachtree, about fifteen hundred square feet of usable space, and rented it for $175 a month. Levy was good at building. He made shelves, designed racks. He hung chains from the ceiling and attached them to steel bars to hang clothes. He stacked goods atop wooden barrels or hung them on metal pipes. He took two wheelbarrows and laid wood across them as a counter. Anything to keep the new place from looking like every old place in town.

Boogie selected the merchandise. He understood fashion in his bones, from a lifetime of watching people with money deck themselves out while he wore his brothers' leftovers. There was one nearby clothing store on Peachtree Street, whose inventory looked to Boogie like holdovers from an earlier era.

"Goodie two-shoes fashions," he said. "I looked in the window and thought they were selling stuff for a bar mitzvah. Preppy stuff. Weejun loafers with pennies, khakis with cuffs, plaid shirts and belts, stuff that the fraternity boys were wearing when I was wearing pants held up with safety pins and they were calling me a dirtball. I was for anything that was anti-fashion, anti-preppy."

He was also nurturing a grudge. His old boss was still cheating him on commissions. "You screw me, I'm gonna screw you back," he says half a century later. So, when they opened the first Merry-Go-Round, he was still collecting pay from Highlander Suede while taking a pass on any actual work for the company. He did this for a couple of months, until it became clear that Merry-Go-Round was a major hit. By then, everybody in town knew it. And the fallout was about to create a whole new life on The Strip.

"The whole street," Levy remembers, "was a mess when we first moved in. Drunks wandered around. It was nothing like it became later. We took three or four months just putting the store together, figuring out all the pieces and the mood and the design."

They brought in half a dozen hippie kids who helped clean and renovate the place. They were young, they embraced the country's growing counter-culture, and they worked hard. In the midst of grueling hours of physical labor, everybody, including

Boogie and Levy, would take a quick break, lean back, smoke a little weed and get high.

One of these hippie kids was a girl named Rhona Pope, an art major at school who danced nights at one of the local clubs. Boogie dated her for a while. Bunch of them were still putting the place together one day, dust flying, hammers banging away, when somebody realized the store still didn't have a name.

"What do we call it?" Boogie wondered aloud.

"I don't know," Rhona said, "but this place is a frickin' merry-go-round. Everything just goes 'round and 'round."

Merry-Go-Round, of course.

It felt like a natural, and it stuck.

When they opened their doors the first day, the action kicked right in, drawn first by music they sent out to the street with loudspeakers. Not Muzak, which put people to sleep, but songs that set a mood. Jose Feliciano singing, "Come on, baby, light my fire," or the Beatles doing some magic carpet ride stuff. People were jitterbugging while they waited in line. When they got inside they found Boogie doing his own dance steps, and boys with long hair, girls in tube tops, waiting to help.

They also saw bell bottom pants, low-rise jeans, floppy hats in different colors. The concrete floor was painted red. There were two-by-four counters supported by fish barrels, and a guy named Ron the Leather Man. He did custom-made sandals with straps while you looked around. He took a pencil and outlined your foot. They saw a classic advertising poster of the era that said, "You don't have to be Jewish to love Levy's Rye Bread." The sign was a natural, with Bob Levy standing right there.

With its Jewish allusion, the sign also hinted at something the country was wrestling with in the anxious post-riot years: ethnic differences, racial tensions. At Merry-Go-Round, they played with these differences instead of shying from them. They'd give a door prize to the tenth black person to walk into the store, or the twelfth woman, or the fifth Asian. Turn all the sensitivities on their heads, make any anxieties a shared laugh. Hey, we're hipper than those other places, we're not even afraid of dirty words. They hung a nonsense sign that said, "Please Don't Phuque with the Pants."

Sometimes the lines outside the store were so long, they'd put up rope and then make it a game to get inside. You'd have to jump the rope to get in, or limbo under it. When they finally got inside, there's Boogie, looking like no other store owner ever seen.

"I'd wear a tank top and platform shoes," he says. "Guys weren't wearing three-inch heels in those days. But I'm thinking, Tom Jones, the singer. He was big back then. I mean, he was five-feet-five, but he had platform shoes that made him look tall. So I picked up on that. Guys come in who were short, I'd sell 'em Verde platform shoes and bell bottoms."

That first Merry-Go-Round opened July 8, 1968, a Friday, and by Sunday they'd sold almost every piece of merchandise. But it wasn't just outfits they were hustling, it was a whole attitude. This is the hangout for anti-fashion. You walk into this funky place, you're joining part of a revolution, looking for a new identity. In Boogie's head, it was also a shout at all those fraternity boys in their straight outfits: you're the losers now, about to feel self-conscious and out of step. I'm the one who was cool all along.

Fashion was about more than clothes now, it was a statement about politics, about morality, about an approach to life itself. Whose side were you on? Those military martinets, setting fire to tiny village huts in Vietnam? Or kids singing, "Give Peace A Chance," while they passed a joint around?

The military types were decked out in uniforms; here, you could buy jeans that were pre-torn. The military types had buzz-cut hair. Here, the hair went on forever. You walked out of Merry-Go-Round and you had more than a new outfit. You'd confirmed an identity, you were kissing off grey conformity, at least until you went back to work.

That first Sunday, with their entire inventory vanishing by the hour, they ordered more clothes, not knowing if they'd arrive in time for a Monday opening.

"Gotta open," Boogie said. "We don't want to be a hippie store. We're in this as a business."

The store stayed open late Sunday night, so Boogie partied around town and then slept in on Monday morning. Levy got up early and went to work. When a delivery truck arrived with boxes of clothes, he called Boogie, still asleep back at the apartment.

"You better get down here," he said. "You won't believe what just arrived."

Their ship had come in.

"We had to close our doors that first weekend," Boogie recalls, "because we were totally sold out. I flew up to New York the next week with my heart pounding, because I knew I had a gold mine."

For the next year, Levy remembers, they turned over their entire inventory every week. Weekends, they had lines around the block, high school kids, college kids, flower children, runaways, suburban home owners who heard young people talking about this crazy place and wanted a piece of the action. Within a year or so, when Boogie went on buying trips, he wasn't just heading for New York. Now it was Los Angeles, too, and then it was all the way to Hong Kong and Taiwan.

"We were in the right place at the right time," Levy says. "The whole country was protesting something, and this was a way to clothe yourself in protest. Old ragtag jeans, and they'd cut 'em and sew flowers on shirts. Then we started doing our own jeans with the rips already built in. That was a statement, too. It was fashionable to be anti-fashion.

"They were buying stuff as fast as we could bring it in. We had trouble finding merchandise, that's how fast it was going out. Male slacks, we had this one place where they had 300 pairs of bell bottoms, and we walked in with $10,000. Guy named Ted Kominsky was head of the company.

"We negotiated for every pair of bell bottoms, at $3 a pair. We paid him in cash. He said, 'You leave me the rest of your money, I'll give you my next cutting.' We said, 'Tell you what. You do your next cutting and we'll come back with the rest of the cash.' He thought we were a couple of hippies. We were really capitalist hippies.

"Boogie had an incredible sense of buying and negotiating. He'd tell me, 'Everything is negotiable, because it's all made up.' And the boutique business, everything was new. We'd buy close-outs up in New York, and take the stuff back to Atlanta, and nobody in the state of Georgia had ever seen anything like it. We'd make 3 or 4 times the markup.

"We'd be opening boxes," Levy says, "and didn't even have time to price 'em. We'd sell for $10 what we bought for $3. We didn't even have time to figure what price to put, they were going so fast. It was such fun, every day I wanted to go to work. And every day I couldn't wait to get down to the store and see who I could hit on. All these teenagers coming in, man…"

They were both single and in their 20s, so the age difference with college girls wasn't exactly vast. On nights when they closed late, an exhausted Levy would usually go back to the apartment to sleep, but Boogie would hit the local clubs. Levy would open up the next day while Boogie slept in, keeping faith with his National Guard vow never to get up too early.

"We'd open at 12 noon," Levy remembers, "and stay open until 2 in the morning. Boogie would walk in at one minute before noon. At midnight, I'd go home and sleep, and he'd go clubbing. Probably to The Scene. And he'd promote the hell out of our business. He'd do contests there. Wet tee shirt contests, best bikini contests. 'We'll supply the bikinis, you supply the girls.' Hottest bikinis you ever saw in your life. And people are loving it, and Merry-Go-Round keeps getting bigger. We had wheelbarrows full of money. We'd walk down the street, I'd carry the money, Boogie carried the gun."

There were occasional bumps in the road. Levy's in the store one day and Boogie's back at the apartment, not yet awake. Some good ol' boy walks in with a shotgun in one hand and his teenage daughter in the other. He points the shotgun at Levy.

"You got my daughter pregnant," the guy says.

"I did not," Levy says.

"No, daddy, not him," the girl says. "It's the other one."

That's one version, anyway. There's an old friend from Baltimore, a refugee from Hilltop Diner days, Larry Oberfeld, who comes down to Atlanta and stays a while. In 1990, GQ Magazine does a huge spread on Boogie, and Oberfeld has his version of the shotgun incident, which fits right into ongoing legend.

"It was wild," Oberfeld told GQ. "The first day I was there, Boogie was fucking this chick behind the furnace. I was with mine in the back of the store." It's a month later, he said, when "the father of the girl came in with a gun, looking for Boogie, yelling, 'He ruined my best young 'un.'"

In either telling of the story, Boogie's not there. Levy calls him at home and tells him about the shotgun-wielding father.

"Give him five grand," Boogie says, though he's not even sure who the girl is. The guy's still ticked off but at least he takes the money and goes away. When Boogie shows up later that day, a friendly cop wanders into the store. They tell him about the confrontation.

"We can't stay here and give you 24-hour a day protection," the cop tells Boogie. "I wouldn't come back in the store for a while."

"You mean, an hour or two?"

"No, a week or two."

Fortunately, Boogie's got a place to go, for he'd fallen in love a few weeks earlier, in a gesture that would get someone locked up in a more sensitive era. He casually poked his head into a dressing cubicle while a customer was trying on jeans.

Her name was Jane Cisar. She worked as Bunny Nicole at the Playboy Club half a mile from the store. She was blond and statuesque. At first sight, Boogie's so smitten, he walks away from a paying customer. Jane's strictly looking for bell bottoms, only she's too tall for any they've got in stock.

"She came in the store that day and my heart stopped," Boogie recalls.

"I was 18 years old," Jane remembers more than half a century later. She was an army brat who'd just moved to Atlanta from Huntsville, Alabama, and found work at the Playboy Club where Boogie occasionally dropped in after Merry-Go-Round closed for the night.

"I was a hick," she says. "And I walked into Merry-Go-Round, and suddenly I'm in the coolest place in the whole world. And Boogie's next to me, right away, and he pulls out a pair of pants my size and shows me where the changing room is. It wasn't so much a room as a couple of pieces of board on the sides, and a sheet up front. And all of a sudden I look up, and Boogie's on a ladder and he's looking down, asking me if I need any help. I thought, 'How dare him?'"

But, when she emerged, he said they sometimes needed models, and would she be interested? Yes, she would. She gave him her phone number. He called her. It was 3 in the morning. His sense of time was getting a little foggy.

"You want to go out?" he asked.

"Are you crazy?" she said.

"Who is it?" her sister asked from the next bed.

"It's that jerk from the store today."

The next night, though, she showed up at the Playboy Club dressing room with the jeans she'd bought from Boogie. The jeans were a hit with the other bunnies. Some of them started showing up at Merry-Go-Round for their own outfits.

"They'd come back to the club and say they met Boogie," Jane recalls. "They said he was adorable." A few of them failed to mention they gave Boogie their phone numbers.

But he kept calling Jane for a date until she said yes. Took her to an Iron Butterfly concert, got front row seats, then took her dancing. They kept going out. She found herself falling in love, though she never fully trusted him. She always wondered who else he was dating. There were others, but he hadn't been in love like this since he married Joanie.

So there he was, with this Atlanta cop telling him to stay out of the store for a week or so until the guy with the shotgun and pregnant daughter cooled off. Where could he stay? He went straight to Jane's apartment, where he stayed for two weeks.

"He was there so long," Jane recalls, "he was wearing my underwear. He hadn't brought any of his own. And he had a doctor's appointment and when they ask him to disrobe, he's wearing my bikini underwear."

Meanwhile, Bob Levy's also fallen hard. Woman walks into the store one day, and Bob's knocked over. But he knows Boogie's already eyeing her.

He whispers, "Boog, lay off."

"I know her," Boogie says.

"I don't care. Have I ever said that to you?"

While Levy's hitting on her, Boogie's taking her money. Later, he tells Levy he short-changed her, just because he was ticked off at Bob for stealing her away. Half a century later, Bob and Vicky are still married. And Boogie and Jane remain close friends over their whole lives.

When Boogie returned from his shotgun-induced sabbatical, business was still terrific. One of the local TV news operations decided here was a great story: not only a hip clothing store, but lines around the block, crazy fashions, lots of young people buying into a new culture.

It was such a good story, the TV people felt, that they sent over one of their news anchors. The guy's a stiff with all the insight of TV's Ted Baxter, the Mary Tyler Moore prototype of every dimwit local anchor in the country.

They set up an interview at the store with the anchor and Boogie, one on one. Boogie's got hair down to his shoulders. The temperature's in the 90s. The anchor's in a suit and tie. Boogie's wearing a tee shirt and jeans and platform shoes with goldfish in the heels. The anchor starts mocking Boogie's outfit on the air. He thinks he'll embarrass him. Boogie takes offense.

"Hey, man," he tells the anchor, "I'm comfortable as shit. You're sweating your ass off."

This is on live television. And, for Merry-Go-Round, it fits the rebel image to a tee.

They even had their own way to deal with trouble-makers. One guy keeps coming into the place just to shoplift. They let him go a few times but told him not to come back. He didn't listen. When they took him to court, the judge fined the jerk $25, not much, and the guy's dumb enough to go back to the store and steal again. And he gets caught again.

"Boogie says to me, 'Hold the gun on this guy.' Then he grabs the guy, one motion, and breaks his arm. We never saw the guy again," Levy says.

Now, just months after they'd opened and word was spreading around Atlanta, there were new businesses opening on the block. Success breeds imitators. The new places had their own funkiness.

"Head shops with pipes and papers came in," Levy remembers, "and a record place, Mother's Music. They started calling the area The Strip. At first, it was just us and three or four other stores. We had Piedmont Park nearby. We had a place called The Catacombs down the street. Hippies hung out at both places.

"After a while, we're pulling in people from all over Georgia and the South. It'd take an hour to drive down that two or three blocks. People in their cars are staring at the hippies and the girls with no bras. Today the kids are wearing tattoos and rings in their noses. Back then it was raggedy looking clothes and sandals."

As the Merry-Go-Round crowds kept expanding, so did The Strip. New stores, more traffic, wider word of mouth. Some of the talk reached all the way back to Baltimore, where Harold Goldsmith picked up the phone one day and called his old friend.

Chapter Ten

"It Was Our Berkley, Our Haight-Ashbury"

The telephone call from Baltimore comes four years after they opened the first Merry-Go-Round on The Strip in Atlanta. By this time, they've expanded the business to four stores, all exploding, stretched along endless Peachtree Street. The phone call comes from Harold Goldsmith. The dialogue remains evergreen in Boogie's mind.

"We just did $4,000 worth of business on a Saturday," he tells Harold.

This is $4,000 in 1972 money, on a blighted stretch previously pronounced dead, which is now swarming with cars, and with foot traffic, and with lines outside Merry-Go-Round and a bunch of quirky new businesses which nobody could have foreseen.

"You're full of shit," says Harold, always quick with numbers, and quick to call out bullshit. "Nobody does that kind of business in a little dump like you got."

"You don't believe me, get on a fuckin' plane and come on down."

Harold hangs up the phone. He keeps telling himself this kind of money is impossible in such a dinky little operation. Harold was down there once already, about a year ago, with his first wife Rona. The place was jumping, all right, but it was so disorganized they didn't even have price tags on the merchandise. When a customer liked something, the sales rep would hold it aloft and holler across the store, "Boog, how much for this?"

Now Boogie's talking about $4,000 in a single day? The same Boogie who used to run from the cops when he and Harold were roommates? Doing this kind of business in Atlanta? Who are his customers, the redneck Georgia descendants of Scarlett and Rhett?

Harold tells himself it's impossible, even as he's picking up the phone again. This time he's making airline reservations for another trip to Atlanta. He doesn't believe Boogie for a moment, yet he keeps thinking about that number - $4,000 in a single day, in a time when some working people don't bring home $4,000 in a year—and Harold's comparing it with his own money.

Yeah, he's doing pretty well. He's still collecting money on the family properties. Plus, he's added a bunch of houses of his own, a slight step up from the homes where he used to collect rent for his father. He hates all of it. Never mind $4,000 in a day, Harold's picking up $25 here, maybe $35 there, only now he's got people mailing in their rent and Rona's handling the books. So, what the hell, he hops on a plane and heads to Atlanta.

Since Harold's no longer around to describe the scene outside Merry-Go-Round at his arrival, let's take a look back from The Great Speckled Bird, that counter-culture weekly newspaper that flourished in Atlanta during this period.

The paper recalls The Strip of this brand new era combining "straight and hip worlds joined in commerce...the marketplace for drugs both benign and harmful…shops with papers, pipes, sandals, literature…zippered boots, tie-dyed shirts, local acts like the Hampton Grease Band, The Sweet Younguns…the colorful kaleidoscope of costumes, the traffic jams, walking out to cars and sharing a joint until the light changed…it's being young, it's refusing to be programmed toward success and money and war. It's daring to seek a new identity."

"When we moved in," Bob Levy says, "there were half a dozen abandoned stores on the block. That's it. It was all derelicts and drunks and hookers. It was desolate. Six months after we got things going, it'd take half an hour to drive down that one block. Everybody showed up. It was our Berkley, our Haight Ashbury."

The Strip has exploded with life, and so has Merry-Go-Round. The fashions are not only subversive, but fun. They're selling platform shoes with coins and clocks in the heels. They've got bell bottom pants Boogie's buying for 50 cents from Navy surplus. He gets them dry cleaned for maybe $1.50 apiece and sells them for $10.

Merry-Go-Round becomes one of the first unisex stores in the whole country. What does Boogie know about women's fashions? Well, he's dating half the females in North America, and they're all wearing miniskirts. You don't have to be some fashionista to get on the phone and tell your manufacturers, "Send more minis—and make 'em micros."

Speaking of which…the young ladies in their minis arrive in endless profusion. Not only daytime at Merry-Go-Round, but nighttime in the lives of Boogie and Levy. In the modern sensibility, it's considered tasteless to mention numbers. But, in December of 1990, in the big piece GQ magazine lavished on him, Boogie addressed the arithmetic.

"It's funny, that came up a couple of months ago," he told GQ. "Like, in the beginning you go through five or ten real quick." He means the tabulating of these intimacies, not the actual women. "And an hour after I finished counting, I thought of another one. You know who I forgot? My first wife."

"Boog, did you hit triple digits?" a friend asks him.

"In a month," he says. Everybody laughs at this. "It's safe to say I was very easy. I admit I was very easy. I definitely set a record for a Jewish guy. Anyone could put me in the sack."

When Harold arrives, the evidence is everywhere: so many beautiful girls waiting along Peachtree Street, he's never seen the likes of it. They've got so many customers lined up, they only let 10 of them in at a time, and then they lock the front door to keep an eye out for shoplifters. (The girl on top of the freezer isn't much help with that.) The line outside never goes away. So Harold's impressed even before he comes in off the street.

Inside, it feels like a carnival. Music's playing, cash register's jingling, Boogie's dancing around. Harold's eyes have never been so wide. He sees airline stewardesses there. He sees college kids, high school hippies. If he sticks around, he'll see rock stars. The great crooner Jackie Wilson's been a customer. So have the Allman Brothers, Ronnie Millsap, Alabama, Richie Havens. Where else would they find outfits this cool? Montgomery Ward's?

Business is so strong, in fact, that by now they've opened a store right across the street. They don't want to compete with themselves, though, so the new place has a whole different sensibility, such as red velvet walls, and a different name: Sexy Sadie's.

"At Sexy Sadie's, we were selling to hookers," Levy says. Also, to the bunnies from the nearby Playboy Club. "It was that kind of an area, hippies and hookers, everybody thrown together. But the stuff that hookers wanted, the girls dressing up for their high school proms wanted the same stuff. Mothers would call and complain. So Boogie got the idea, let 'em bring the stuff back, and we'll mark it down and the hookers will get it at a discount. And most people didn't even know we owned both stores."

But it's Merry-Go-Round that captivates Harold. "He's foaming at the mouth," Boogie recalls. "He's got all these properties up in Baltimore, but he hates it. And now he walks into this place, and he can't believe what he sees."

"Boog," Harold says, "you gotta put this in the malls."

Right away, he's thinking like a partner. Boogie's way ahead of him. He's been trying to get into a couple of shopping malls already, but the owners don't trust him. They see a guy with long hair and torn jeans and platform shoes and figure he'll never pay the rent. And Boogie's refusing to get dressed up just to impress some moron mall manager. So he can't get his foot in the door of any of those places.

Harold's thinking: Yeah, but I could.

Nobody's going to mistake him for anything less than what he's always been: a serious adult, a smart guy in a suit, a fellow who greets each bright new day looking to make all the money in the whole world.

As everybody knows, he's got the brains for it. Skipped a couple of grades in school, he was so smart and so serious. That's why he was always one of the younger guys at the Hilltop Diner. Barely past his bar mitzvah, he was already in high school. Went to City College, got out early.

At the diner, guys were cutting up, and Harold was as sarcastic any of them. But he was thinking beyond the next smile. Some guys sat down talking about how far they got with this girl or that one, and he's questioning them like they're on a witness stand. Some of the guys, they make sure Harold's not around before they start doing any bragging. He takes a grin and analyzes the crap out of it.

He picks up a nickname: Oliver, or Ollie. The guys figure it's the perfect name for a nerd. A math nerd, at that. He knows numbers like nobody else. Go ahead, ask him 75 times 43, he can do it in his head.

That first day in Atlanta, he can't believe how high the numbers go. Boogie remembers they did $5,500 that day. Harold's so impressed, he decides to stay a couple of days. Around 11 that first night, they're walking up Peachtree Street to Boogie's nearby apartment when Boogie senses they're being followed by a couple of toughs.

"Let's cross here," he says.

"Why here?"

"Just follow me."

The two toughs follow them across.

"I got scared," says Boogie, recalling the night so many years later, "because Harold couldn't fight, and he couldn't run, either. I knew they wanted to mug us, because we'd just left the store."

Boogie and Harold don't look so tough. They're both under six feet, and they're both skinny. The two attackers have come armed.

"I'm gonna stay here and talk to these guys," Boogie tells Harold. "You go up the next block, and when I start to run to you, I want you to run in the front door."

Harold's happy to go ahead and wait outside the apartment building. Boogie pauses as the tough guys make their approach. It's a hot summer night. He glances up the street and sees Harold wave at him to show he's safe. Here come the tough guys.

"Listen guys, I'm not looking for any trouble," he tells them. They pause for an instant. But now one of them splits off, out into the street. The guy approaching Boogie has his hand behind his back, and Boogie can see what he's got there: a large rock. He's looking to clock Boogie in the head while the other fellow jumps in from behind.

So it's a little late for words.

"I threw my right hand at the guy with the rock," Boogie recalls. "He wasn't ready. Caught him beautiful. He drops the rock, and now I hit him with a left. He goes down. To make sure, I took my knee as he's going down, and I hit him so hard I almost broke my knee. He's out cold, fell off the curb into the street. I turn to the other guy, who sees what happened and starts to run. I ran after him for about 30 yards and stopped. If I didn't have cowboy boots on, I'd have caught him."

Now he leans over the guy in the street, who's starting to stir. "Buddy, don't get up," Boogie tells him. "If you do, you're going back down."

With that, he walks toward his apartment, where he sees Harold waving his arms around like crazy and hollering in a deep guttural voice that nobody's ever heard coming out of Harold before this.

"Yeah, Boog, yeah!"

He's celebrating, he's screaming, he's jumping up and down. Couple of cars are slowing to see what's going on. Harold can't believe what a day it's been, all that business at the store, and now this triumph in the street.

They get upstairs to Boogie's place, and Harold says, "You know what? You ought to let me buy in."

"And this," Boogie says half a century later, "is how Harold became my partner."

But it's also the beginning of the end for Bob Levy. The two of them, Harold and Levy, hate each other right away. The hatred starts even before Harold's arrival in Atlanta. A year earlier, with Merry-Go-Round bursting its seams, and four new stores spread along Peachtree Street, the boys decide to open a store in Towson, just north of Baltimore.

What the hell, Boogie's brother Eggy needs a job. They'll let him run the place. He'd already spent some time in Atlanta, learning the ropes, picking up the vibe, and only occasionally getting himself into trouble.

Boogie put him to work as a salesman. Eggy tended toward slight impatience. One time, he watched a customer take forever to make her selection.

"Can I help you with anything?" he asked.

"I'm just looking," the woman responded.

"Well, why don't you just go outside and look through the window?" Eggy said.

Despite his short fuse, when they put Eggy in charge of the Towson store, he did pretty well with it. The store's thriving, and Eggy's finally got some financial stability. He's still got some gambling issues, handed down genetically from Solomon. But he's got some solid ground to stand on in the store. Eggy looks up to his younger brother. They're bonding as never before. Plus, it doesn't hurt, a few years later, when Boogie buys Eggy a brand new yellow Mercedes.

The Towson store's memorable for one other thing. It's where Bob Levy and Harold Goldsmith first met. Bob went up for the opening. As a Merry-Go-Round partner, he was there to look at the layout and get all the insurance work straightened out. Harold was there mainly to annoy Bob.

"Boogie said he's a friend, that's all I knew," Levy remembers. "He starts telling me how things ought to be run. At this point, he wasn't involved at all, and we're feeling like rock stars, we're so successful. We had money rolling in, and customers lined up. And he's telling me how to run my operation. It took me less than an hour to realize I hated him."

Then comes Harold's arrival in Atlanta, a year later, where the hatred gets worse.

"You don't need that hillbilly," Harold tells Boogie.

"I don't like that guy," Bob tells Boogie. "I couldn't work with him."

"Bob, I need him," Boogie tells him.

"Boogie was talking about moving to Baltimore," Levy remembers. "Hell, I wasn't going to move up there. They'd been through riots, the place looked like a bomb hit. Atlanta, the quality of life was great. I'd just bought a lake-front house. And I couldn't stand Harold."

Boogie understood. He knew Harold could be tough to like. He was okay until you disagreed with him, and then he tended to explode.

"I weighed the emotional stuff," Boogie recalls. "Harold wasn't a bad guy, but he wasn't easy. But we were roommates when Joanie and me broke up, and that counted. He gave me a place to stay. I was grateful, and I felt indebted. He couldn't fight or dance, but he wasn't a bad guy."

Also, he knew nothing about fashion. "It was embarrassing, the way he dressed," Boogie said. "Khakis, pants the wrong length. He could walk in the gutter and not get his pants wet." But he knew business, and he had some sense of real estate.

Harold offers a deal. He'll give Boogie half interest in all his rental properties up in Baltimore. There are nearly a hundred of them by now. In exchange, he'll take half interest in any Merry-Go-Round stores they develop together.

That last part is the key. Harold's been talking Boogie's ear off about shopping malls. He's got some real estate savvy, and he dresses like a grown-up, and he believes shopping malls are the Promised Land. Never mind Atlanta, he thinks he can take Merry- Go-Round everywhere. Boogie, never one to think small, loves what he hears. But he's torn, because he and Levy have been through a lot, and they're pals. But Levy's insistent.

"I can't work with this guy," he says.

So the two old partners work out a deal which, to this day, Levy calls amicable. He gets all four Atlanta stores, and Boogie and Harold get the Merry-Go-Round name. The brand—and Boogie's sense of fashion, his seat-of-the-pants flair - is the heart of it.

Levy stays in Atlanta, where he meets the woman who walks into the store to buy clothes and leaves holding Levy's heart. They're married for the rest of their lives. Levy expands the business modestly, but successfully.

"I had some hard feelings at the time," he says in reflection. "But I didn't see what was coming with Merry-Go-Round—hell, nobody could—so I take responsibility. But those years were fabulous, and I learned a ton from Boogie.

"You know, my dad was a New York City fireman. I was a job guy, that's all. Boogie opened my eyes. He taught me you could dream. So I got the Atlanta stores, which I expanded to 11 stores at one point, and then I burned out. I'm not a day-to-day guy. I put my friends in business, and then I sold out to them.

"But those years with Boogie—well, I never had so much fun in my life. He's the most amazing person I ever met, utterly fearless, utterly generous."

And he was just getting started.

Chapter Eleven

The Odd Couple

Everybody who knows Boogie and Harold calls this the oddest coupling of all time. The wise guys from the old days at the Hilltop Diner and Benny's have spread out now, joining the exodus to suburban Pikesville and Owings Mills and Randallstown. But they all agree on one thing: at any given moment, Boogie and Harold will turn each other into nuclear dust.

Boogie can't put his hands on money without dispensing it like he's Earl Monroe dishing out assists. Sometimes he's bankrolling old Baltimore friends who have run into bumpy times. Sometimes he's gambling on ballgames. It's a growing passion as his wallet fattens. Sometimes, as business shifts into Baltimore and he thinks about the years of scuffling, he's spending money just to make up for lost time.

When the big bucks start piling up faster than he can spend them, he moves into the Hopkins House building, just off University Parkway, down the block from the Johns Hopkins University. He doesn't just rent an apartment. He rents the big building's entire top floor. He buys a Rolls-Royce and happily pays cash for it. When he needs a second car, he gets himself a limousine, and then two. He uses one for his mother.

"Send the station vagon around," Nettie says. That's what she calls the limo, "the station vagon."

By this time, he's set his mother up in a swell new apartment in a nice neighborhood. He pays her rent, naturally—and pays the rent for the rest of their lives for several of her closest friends, as well. And he takes care of Nettie's clothes. She won't let him buy expensive stuff, so he goes to the dress store where she shops, and has them mark down the prices so she'll get them. And then he secretly pays the full price for her.

He's taken care of his brothers, too. He's got Eggy running the Towson store, and he's set up Jackie. Boogie does Merry-Go-Round's buying, so he tells a few suppliers, "We'll buy from you, but I need my brother Jackie to handle the lines."

As one more testament to the good life, Boogie hires a huge fellow named Ralph Banner. Ralph will spend the next 15 years as Boogie's man on call, his fulltime chauffeur and bodyguard, his best friend, his penthouse mate atop Hopkins House, and co-best man at Boogie's second wedding.

Harold's approach to life is a little different than Boogie's.

When he and Boogie join forces, Harold's already making pretty good money with his row-house rental properties. But he tends to spend like Scrooge McDuck. Newly wed, he and his bride honeymoon in Florida. They go by train, which is cheaper than flying. Cheaper yet, they stay in Florida with Harold's parents.

"Every girl's dream, honeymooning with the in-laws," recalls the former Rona Yaffe Goldsmith.

But it's precisely that chemical mix that makes the two men mesh. Let Boogie with his fashion instincts and his unchained id pick out the tattered jeans and the tee shirts and miniskirts. "We're selling sex and hipness," he says. Let Harold deal with the accountants and their dreary rows of numbers and the uptight managers in charge of the shopping malls.

"The game plan," Boogie recalls decades later, "was to go into regional malls. The way I looked, the way I dressed, I wasn't too good with mall managers. They thought I looked like a second-class drug dealer. Harold wanted me to get dressed, wear a suit, cut my hair. That was never gonna work.

"So he said, 'Okay, let me deal with the suits. You deal with the fashions.' He got me great locations, and I filled them up with the best fuckin' shit. I just had the knack of buying unique stuff, and he was content opening malls. And we're knocking the cover off the ball."

They open Merry-Go-Rounds at Security Square Mall and Westview Mall. Both are located in suburban Baltimore, several miles from the city's lingering anxieties. It's 1972, four years after the riots, but Baltimore's still living under emotional shadows.

The city's leaking population. Downtown after dark is a ghost town, and residential neighborhoods across Baltimore are emptying out. In 1960, the city's population is nearly 1 million; it's America's 6th biggest city. By 1970, two years after the riots, barely 900,000 remain. A decade later, the number's dropped below 800,000 and heading much lower still.

The '68 riots will change the city of Baltimore forever. This is only a single piece of the American payback, not only for the murder of Martin Luther King, but for generations of blacks treated like second-class human beings. In Baltimore, in those four days and nights of rage, the rioters set more than twelve hundred buildings afire. It takes more than twelve thousand U.S. soldiers to try to calm the city.

At the height of the insanity, with a curfew imposed, armed troops gathered at the city's Fifth Regiment Armory, where their commander, African-American, instructed them, "If anybody's walking, you order them to halt. If they don't stop the first time, you order them to halt a second time. If he don't stop the second time, shoot him."

Behind him, the commander heard a couple of civilians gasp at his words. One of them was Marvin Mandel, soon to become governor of Maryland. Years later, Mandel remembered the commander whipping around and declaring, "Let me tell you something. See all these men in this company? They've survived fighting in Vietnam. And I'm not going to let them get killed on the streets of Baltimore."

It takes years to shed images of a city on fire, with the shattered glass of store fronts covering the streets, and furious people lashing out. Many families aren't waiting around to see if the town will cool off. The second big post-war exodus is now swirling, and by the early '70s it takes away almost all the old familiar places.

The Hilltop Diner's about to close its doors after a quarter-century run. Mandell's Deli has a well-timed kitchen fire, covered by insurance, and doesn't re-open. Their old customers have fled to the aptly named Suburban House and the food courts at malls. The Crest Theater and the other northwest Baltimore movie palaces are only a few heartbeats from shutting down, and the pools rooms at Benny's and Knocko's are gone.

For generations, the heart of retail shopping for Baltimoreans—especially whites—was downtown's Howard Street corridor. There you found the department store behemoths, Hutzler's, Hochild Kohn's, Stewarts, Brager-Gutman, The May Co.

When you went to Howard Street, it felt like an occasion. The women wore hats and high heels, and the men wore coats and ties. Nobody wanted to look like a shlepper. They dressed as though they were meeting the vice president of Union Trust.

By '72, though, all these Howard Street stores were either dying or dead. They closed their doors and followed their customers to the suburbs where the stores were born again inside the brand new shopping malls.

Esquire Magazine said these malls spread across America "like fungi, unstoppable in their growth and unbeatable for their earning power. By the mid-Seventies there were more than 15,000 shopping malls in America, hauling in more than $150 billion worth of business."

Inside the malls, there was no more trudging through the cold, or the heat, the way it was all those years along the Howard Street corridor. The new malls were air conditioned, and heated, and they had impregnable walls. Shoppers felt safe in these places.

Security Square Mall had a built-in audience for Merry-Go-Round. Not only were there surrounding residential neighborhoods, and nearby Woodlawn High with its teenagers hungry to look cool, but just up Security Boulevard was the Social Security Administration where tens of thousands of workers gathered every day and took home middle class paychecks.

It didn't take the two local boys, Boogie and Harold, very long to figure out the best places to locate—and Baltimore's buying patterns were similar everywhere they looked across the whole country.

Now that Boogie was back home, he sensed some of his old resentments return. Those rich-boy fraternity brats of yesteryear thought they were dressed so well? Now he'd show them how un-hip they really were. He'd show everybody that the tattered jeans and the tee shirts like he once wore were the cool way to dress, and always had been.

But he wasn't buying just to outfit his own resentments. He was offering hints of James Dean in "Rebel Without A Cause," or Bob Dylan singing, "Twenty years of schooling/And they put you on the day shift."

Or maybe this was closer to "The Wild One," where the hot chick asks Marlon Brando, "What are you rebelling against, Johnny?"

"What have you got?" he replies.

At Merry-Go-Round, you could shop in the bourgeois heart of the suburban middle class—the shopping mall - and yet feel you were kissing off the straight life a little bit. You could still go to high school and prep for your SAT exams—but you could show up in homeroom wearing torn jeans as a signal to your classmates that you weren't buying into all the bullshit the grownups were trying to force-feed you.

"It was absolutely a statement," Boogie says. "It was anti-preppy, anti-fashion. I was against anything that looked like Weejun loafers with pennies, khakis with cuffs, plaid shirts and belts. I was still angry about all the fraternity boys wearing preppy clothes and I was a dirtball to them. This was all about people telling me what to do, how to dress. It was absolutely anti-straight society."

Slipping past 30 now but still nurturing his inner teen and all its resentments, Boogie's got the fashions down. And Harold's running to every mall manager he can find, and he's negotiating all the bank financing.

He makes contact with executives at the Rouse Company, which is charting its own legend across urban America. The company's founder, James Rouse, will find himself on the cover of Time, when such a thing counted as serious cultural impact. The company builds Faneuil Hall in Boston. They build Harborplace in Baltimore. Hell, they build the entire city of Columbia, out in Howard County, including the Columbia Mall where Merry-Go-Round will plant one of its flags.

They've also got malls in Philadelphia, Pittsburgh, and Maryland's Eastern Shore, where Harold secures early leases. And Westview Mall in suburban Baltimore, and malls in Cincinnati and Memphis. Every one's a gold strike, and every gold strike's a message to every mall where Harold makes a future approach: these guys can earn money for you.

"After a while," Boogie recalls, "the malls were chasing us."

Sometimes they're both on the road. When Boogie's in some faraway outpost looking at merchandise to purchase, and Harold's checking out locations, he'll telephone Boogie in some distant state to say, "Can you look at the malls there? Check the traffic, check the layout. You can't just look at blueprints." He values Boogie's instincts.

But Boogie wants no parts of Harold's instincts on fashion. The guy can't dress himself, how's he going to pick fashions for customers? One time, when the money's rolling in so nicely that they each take end-of-year million-dollar bonuses, Harold shows interest in doing a little buying.

"Harold, if you do, I'll break your nose," Boogie tells him. "You do any buying, I'll break your whole fuckin' head."

"I wasn't gonna," Boogie admits decades later. "But that's how bad Harold's taste was."

So Harold leaves it to Boogie to corner the market on each new fashion fad. Once, Boogie finds out the jeans manufacturer Faded Glory's suffering cash-flow problems, so he buys its entire jeans inventory. That's 300,000 pair of jeans. He picked them up for about $5 a pair. Merry-Go-Round sells them for triple the cost.

He's a great one for thinking big, for asking, "How much will it cost if I take everything you have?"

When they open Merry-Go-Round in Memphis, it brings an unanticipated smile. In the early years, any time they open a new location, Boogie arrives to train the managers and the sales reps. He puts ads in the local newspapers: "Coming Tomorrow, America's Hottest Boutique." He sets up interviews with local TV stations. Those folks are always looking to show off characters, and Boogie fits the bill.

In the week Memphis opens, they're hit by a tidal wave of customers. They're lined up along the mall's interior. It's so hectic, Boogie stays around to work the floor until closing time. He's calling Harold every other hour, it's so busy.

The second day they're open, here comes the most beautiful lady Boogie's ever seen. Classy, too, classy enough that he tells her his name is Lenny. She's too classy for a Boogie. She's picking up close to $2,000 worth of stuff. He keeps thinking, where has he seen this gorgeous creature before this?

As she checks out, he goes back to help another customer since the store's so busy. But, as she leaves, carrying half a dozen bags, he offers to help her to her car. Maybe he can get her name and phone number to ask her out. She's driving a Cadillac convertible with the top down and a red interior. Then he notices her license plate. It says, "Elvis."

"Thanks, Lenny," says Priscilla Presley, driving off. "I love your store."

Within one year of the first Merry-Go-Round, they've got 30 stores in various states. In quick order, they've got 60. They build corporate offices in the Baltimore suburb of Owings Mills and a massive warehouse in Towson. The warehouse is so big, Boogie outfits himself with roller skates so he can glide down the endless aisles.

By this time, he's grown a mustache, his hair's down to his shoulders, and he's showing up for work in torn jeans, a girl's knit top, and platform shoes several inches high.

One time, he's on a buying trip to New York and walks into the Calvin Klein showroom in a tee shirt and jeans. Some rep in a high-fashion suit's ready to throw him out of the place, strictly on appearance. So Boogie goes around him.

He calls a Calvin Klein vice president named Carl Rosen. He wants to buy a stockpile of jeans, although—this being Boogie—in the back of his mind, he's also hoping to meet Brooke Shield, the actress who's their company fashion model.

"My name's Leonard Weinglass," he tells Rosen. "Don't judge me by my outfit. I have 200 stores."

"I don't care what you look like if you have 200 stores," Rosen says.

Boogie tells him he wants to buy some Calvin Klein jeans but doesn't like the way they're cut.

"They're made for heffers," he says, "for mature women. Brook Shield isn't heavy set, but that's who you're advertising. They're too big for my clientele. I deal with teens, I deal with the mother who wants to look 16. Your Calvins don't fit the way I want. We're known for sex, and hipness, and your jeans don't work for me."

He shows Rosen a tight-fitting jean that's popular with the Merry-Go-Round crowd. "If you can make a jean with this cut…" he says. "Girls love low-rise, which accents their butt and shows their tummy. Your zipper's too high."

"We'd have to use a whole new mold," Rosen says. "That takes time."

"I can give you a lot of business," Boogie says.

"Will you buy 2,000 pair of jeans to start?"

The first order of 2,000 pairs of the new jeans disappears from Merry-Go-Rounds everywhere in about a week.

When Boogie calls Rosen back, he says, "We're having a little luck with the jeans. I want to order 12,000 more of them. And give me some in black, some in denim, and I want you to put a little fray in the jean, a little tear."

Torn jeans, the kind Boogie used to wear when they called him a dirtball.

Over the next year, Merry-Go-Round sells more than 100,000 pair of those jeans, and 150,000 more over the following year. Everybody's trying to look anti-establishment.

"Boogie had one great talent," says Joe Blumberg. He spent years at Merry-Go-Round, most of them traveling around the country on buying trips with Weinglass. "We'd go into a showroom and they'd have 50 samples that they're showing the public. He could look at a hundred-piece line and find the best thing. And he was always right. It was uncanny. Very few people have that ability. He has fashion sense. What he bought is what he liked to wear. That's against the standard rules of buying. But he made it work."

Blumberg was there when Weinglass was walking the fine professional line between his outer Leonard and his inner Boogie.

"We'd travel together on buying trips," Blumberg says. "I'd dress like Boogie, jeans and a tee shirt and a baseball cap. But I'm holding a $500-million dollar pencil" with which he writes orders.

One Friday afternoon in Baltimore, Boogie tells Blumberg, "We gotta go to Dallas, Blum. This weekend's the swimwear show. They'll have beautiful girls. Let's go."

Blumberg tries to be the grown-up in the room. "Can't do it," he says. "We've got a board of directors meeting here Monday."

"We'll be back in time," Boogie assures him.

"Boogie rents half the floor of the best hotel in Dallas," Blumberg recalls. "We're there for four days, and it's wall-to-wall women with us. We're coming back from dinner one night, and Boogie's wearing a baseball cap with wings on both sides, like the god Mercury. It's this high-class hotel lobby. And Boogie's walking through the place on his hands. The manager wants to arrest him. I tell him, 'Sir, this is Mr. Weinglass, who owes you $70,000.' He says, 'Well, could you just have him calm down a little?'

"We were a couple of days too late for the board of directors meeting. Harold was so freaked out, he hired a detective. He thought we were kidnapped."

He pursues the ladies at these shows, but he does his homework, too. He looks at everything, and he knows a winner when he sees one.

Two years after they break into malls, the whole country's going through a bad economy. It's 1974, the year of the Arab oil embargo, and endless gas lines where fights are breaking out among frustrated drivers, and people are finicky about wasting precious gas just to go to some suburban mall.

The guys' egos are a little tattered, as well. When they're both in town, Harold shows up at the office around 8 in the morning. Boogie's just getting home by then, after nights running around to different clubs. They hang in, because each knows the strengths the other brings. But their nerve endings are getting as frayed as the jeans they're hustling.

"In a million years, Harold wouldn't have been in the clothing business," says Rona Smith, Harold's first wife. She was there during the first 14 years of the Merry-Go-Round partnership. "It was really Boogie who made it work. I mean, they both had the quick tempers. Boogie was always doing something Harold didn't like, and maybe the reverse. But they complemented each other perfectly in business."

When other companies were floundering in the mid-'70s, Merry-Go-Round made it safely through. They changed precisely as the pop culture changed.

They scored big when Boogie latched onto pre-washed jeans as a back-to-school fashion. By 1977, when the country was hit by disco-mania and "Saturday Night Fever," they brought in leisure suits and silk shirts, and three-piece polyester suits and slinky wraparound dresses.

A few years later, as their teenage customers became transfixed by MTV and Michael Jackson appeared with his bright red V-shaped leather jacket with 27 zippers, Merry-Go-Round sold more than 50,000 similar jackets. After "Urban Cowboy" hit movie screens, they brought in Western wear with suede jackets with fringes

By now they were headed toward a hundred stores, and then doubled that number a few years later, and kept doubling every few years. By 1983, barely a decade after they opened the Merry-Go-Round chain, the company went public.

It's a fabulously successful initial offering. Boogie and Harold each make about $13 million on it. They've also gotten so big, they've brought in help at the top, a fellow named Mike Sullivan who'll help run the company. In short order, Sullivan figures it's time to take the company in a new direction.

"If there are, say, 500 great malls in the country," Sullivan tells Baltimore Magazine, "you can only have 500 stores. But if you've got three great divisions, then you can have fifteen hundred stores."

Fifteen hundred stores is precisely where the company's headed at its peak. And so, with the public offering, Merry-Go-Round starts targeting new customers with new types of stores. They launch DJ's for young men, Cignal for maturing male and female baby boomers, and Attivo for men. Then they launch DeJaiz, Silverman's, His Place, Go Places, The Go Round. Eventually, Sullivan will reorganize the company into three divisions, each with its own staff and president.

And Boogie, restless as ever, will head west to Aspen, where he'll open a place called Boogie's Diner, which takes on a life of its own.

Photographs

The Weinglass men when it was all beginning. That's (l to r) Jack, Boogie and Eggy, with dad Solomon. Though Solomon departed early, he left behind a lesson in how to throw a punch.

Weinglass attempts to take ball from Patterson foe.

In his days playing high school basketball for Baltimore City College, Boogie was an All-Star guard who played his way into the school's athletic Hall of Fame.

Mrs. Leonard M. Weinglass

Mr. and Mrs. Jack D. Sutton,
816 Sturgis Place, Pikesville, an-
nounce the marriage of their
daughter. Joan Arlene, to Mr.
Leonard Michael Weingl---

Joanie Sutton was still a teenager when she and Boogie fell in love.
The marriage ended, but not her affection for Boogie.

Boogie in the Sixties, when the wild and crazy days were just
beginning.

Jack, Eggy, Boogie and in front, Louise and mom Nettie Weinglass

It was famed director Barry Levinson who first delivered "Boogie" to the whole country, in "Diner," the coming-of-age film about Baltimore's Hilltop Diner. Mickey Rourke played the young Boogie.

Bob Levy (here with wife Ginger) was Boogie's partner and best pal when they opened their first little boutique in Atlanta and called it Merry-Go-Round.

Harold Goldsmith (back row, center) was the real estate genius who put Merry-Go-Round into shopping malls all over America while Boogie was the fashion guru. They were the Lennon and McCartney of the retail industry.

It was Boogie's mother, Nettie, who kept the family together through the tough years. Whenever Boogie sent a limo for her, Nettie called it "the station wagon."

Ralph Banner was co-best man at Boogie's second wedding, as well as his apartment mate, chauffeur, best friend, and (when needed) protector.

Boogie with some Baltimore pals (l to r) Eddie Jacobson, Sylvan Feldman, Ron Matz, Allan Charles, Ray Altman, Boogie, Leonard Grossman, Stewart Levitas.

The executive at work: Merry-Go-Round's warehouse was so enormous, Boogie wore roller skates to zip his way along the aisles. The headgear was an added touch of playfulness.

A man and his motorcycle. The cycle's not leaving the showroom floor, but it's not a bad metaphor for Boogie's seat-of-the-pants lifestyle.

Boogie's Diner attracted a wide and eclectic crowd, from Goldie Hawn and Donald Trump to Chris Evert and former U.S. Secretary of State Madeline Albright, here with Boogie and wife Gail.

When the town of Aspen needed a new fire truck, it was Boogie who wrote a check for $126,000.

Boogie's Diner was such a triumph, Donald Trump tried to buy his way into the franchise and bring it to New York. Boogie was way ahead of the future President.

Boog with his kids (l to r) Bo, Sage and Skye.

Arms extended for the full embrace of his Aspen empire, Boogie bestrides his diner and the retail store below.

Stairway for the star – Boogie on the staircase dividing Boogie's Diner and the clothing store below.

Boogie and second wife Pepper, the mother of (l to r) Sage, Skye and Bo. The marriage ended after a few decades, but not the mutual affection.

Boogie with grandsons Bravery and Braxton.

Wife Gail with grandsons Braxton and Bravery, their mom Sage, and Boogie.

"This boy can boogie." The dance floor was the birthplace for a nickname that's lasted a lifetime. On this night, they're dancing at Merry-Go-Ranch, Boogie and Gail's Aspen home.

Turning 80, Boogie's a man in repose, reflective on his life's journey and still hugely generous toward those who need a helping hand.

Chapter Twelve

"Are You Any Good at Softball?"

Mike Sullivan comes out of Chicago's South Side, a working class kid who paid his way through college laboring for an oil delivery company. A tough Irish Catholic working with a couple of high-strung Jewish guys, what could possibly go wrong?

But religion's the least of it. The company's growing so fast, Boogie and Harold realize they need more brain power at the top. Sullivan's got a business degree from Loyola University of Chicago. He's had executive jobs with an accounting firm and a cement manufacturer. Now he's treasurer of the Steak and Ale restaurant chain. But he wants to be somebody's CEO one day.

He gets a call from a head-hunter. Company called Merry-Go-Round's looking for a chief financial officer, he's told. Sullivan's never heard of the company. The head-hunter tells him they're growing fast, but they've got a thin management team, and they want to go public. Sullivan thinks this sounds promising. The head-hunter agrees, but with reservations.

The two owners, he explains, tend to look at the same precise things and take precisely different perspectives—particularly, when it comes to human beings.

The first time Sullivan meets Harold, he believes he's never in his whole life met anyone so hyper. More than a decade later, he tells a Baltimore Magazine writer, Anne Bennett Swingle, "Harold had the shortest attention span. He would say a couple of sentences, and then you knew his mind was gone."

"We've got the concept, the merchandising talent, and the real estate," Harold tells Sullivan, "but we need someone to pull the system together. We can't even get our financial statements out on time. We've had three comptrollers in here, and we're still late."

Sullivan goes all the way back to his home base, the Steak and Ale in Dallas, where he gets a phone call from Harold. Can he come back to Baltimore to meet his partner?

"Why didn't we do this when I was in Baltimore?" Sullivan asks, more than slightly ticked off.

"Well," Harold explains, "it's a long story."

As Boogie tells the story, he gets a call from Harold. "I want you to interview this guy Mike Sullivan," he says. "I brought him back to town from Dallas. I think he's our new CFO."

"Okay," Boogie says. "When?"

"Tonight," Harold says.

"Can't do it," Boogie says, "Tonight I'm going to the Orioles game. I got tickets. Right off third base."

"God damn it, call him anyway."

Harold prevails. Boogie calls Sullivan and asks, "You like baseball?"

"I love baseball," Sullivan says. "I play it down in Texas."

As Sullivan will tell the tale, in his memoir, "It's Been A Great Ride," his interview with Boogie is unlike any other he endures, before or since. Remember, this is the co-owner of a serious business looking for a chief financial officer. Sullivan's wearing a suit and tie. Boogie's wearing jeans and a woman's low-cut V-neck tee shirt. He's got a beard. He asks a few questions about Steak and Ale and cash management.

Then he says, "Can I ask you a really important question?"

"Sure," Sullivan says, bracing himself. "What is it?"

"Are you any good at softball?"

This is Weinglass expressing his inner Boogie: Life is more than just making money. The question also reflects a growing restlessness he's feeling, which will soon express itself quite dramatically.

"Why do you ask?" says a puzzled Sullivan.

Boogie doesn't get into philosophy here. He merely explains that he still considers himself a pretty competitive athlete. He mentions his playing days on the basketball court and the baseball field. He declares he was considered "the best Jewish athlete in town" during his days at Forest Park High and City College.

Merry-Go-Round has a company softball team, he says, and they're a disgrace.

"I've decided," Boogie tells Sullivan, "that everybody I hire has to be a good softball player. Are you any good?"

"Yeah, I'm pretty good," Sullivan says.

"Give me some credentials."

Sullivan lays out his ball playing career stretching all the way back to Little League and Babe Ruth League and American Legion ball. He says he played for a White Sox development team until he hurt his shoulder. He boasts that his Steak and Ale teams won league titles, and his church team reached tournament level every year.

"Do you have any press clippings on all that stuff?" Boogie asks.

"No," Sullivan says. "If there were any press clippings, my mother would have had them, and she's been dead for over 10 years."

"Okay," says Boogie, "that's good enough for me." He walks Sullivan over to Goldsmith's office, and announces, "Harold, I love this guy. We've got to hire him."

"Boogie, you can't say that right in front of him," Harold cries. "You just eliminated our bargaining power."

This sets off an argument, with Sullivan standing there in full astonishment. The argument lasts at least five minutes. It ends when Boogie declares, "We're going to hire him, but with one provision. If he's lying about softball, we can fire him with no severance."

"That's the dumbest thing I have ever heard you say," Harold says. "You can't say that to an executive."

"Are you all right with that?" Boogie asks Sullivan.

"I'm all right with that," Sullivan replies.

So he's hired. What's more, he plays a good game of softball. "He bullshitted me how good he was," Boogie claims years later. "He was okay, but not in my class as an athlete."

The job interview's a Boogie classic, but it's part of a culture he's adopted at every level of the business. They've got all kinds of street-corner kids as customers, so why not hire them as well?

One guy who sits for an interview hasn't worked in the last 18 months. Boogie asks what he's been doing all that time.

"Oh, hanging out," the guy says. So Boogie presses him, and finally gets the truth. The guy was doing a little prison time for drug dealing.

"Okay," Boogie tells him, "as long as you're honest in telling me things like that, we'll get along fine."

As Boogie later relates the story to Mat Edelson, at Baltimore Magazine, the guy spent more than a decade at Merry-Go-Round and wound up in management.

"We had a lot of people, just because their hair was a little long or they wore an earring, they couldn't get a job with IBM. They found a home at Merry-Go-Round."

As did Sullivan, whose arrival couldn't be better timed. Not just for softball, but for Sullivan. Boogie's not yet 35, but he's already pondering retirement, not wishing to be one of those drudges who spends all his years joylessly accumulating money while missing an actual life.

Harold's thinking about new ways of minting money. He'll buy himself a Baltimore bank. Then he's eyeing a hostile take-over of a Las Vegas casino. The two of them will stay on the Merry-Go-Round board for some time, but their restlessness means more responsibility, and more muscle, for Sullivan.

Right away, he discovers a corporate culture more casual than anything he's ever seen. Take the company phone directory—everybody's alphabetized by first name. Take the hiring culture—they go for "street kids," not "suits." Check the fashions they choose—they go with Boogie's ever-unfailing gut, not market research.

Those fashions include the tight-fitting parachute pants Michael Jackson wore, and Madonna bustiers, and a knock-off of the leather jacket Jackson wore in his "Thriller" video. Their original cost was $750 per Jackson jacket, which they'd sell for $1,500—about five times higher than anything else in the store. But then they found a Korean vendor who said he could make the same jacket in polyurethane. This one cost Merry-Go-Round $15 apiece, and they sold them for $99. They sold out.

When Sullivan first arrived, Boogie and Harold had already hooked into TV ads. They signed on with Allan Charles, the same fellow Boogie protected from the drapes back at City College. Charles was now a founding partner in the hippest advertising firm in town—Trahan, Burden and Charles, later called TBC—and convinced the new Merry-Go-Round triumvirate to advertise on MTV, which was hypnotizing millions of adolescents across the country.

Charles promised they'd make commercials that would look like music videos. He said they should cut a three-year deal at $1 million a year, pretty big money for the mid-'70s, big enough that Harold heard the figures and exploded. Whoever heard of spending this kind of money?

Boogie, never shy about spreading money around, sees it as a chance to get in on the ground floor. Sullivan agrees. Charles, who knows the TV ad business better than either of them, handles production.

The ad started running a week before Thanksgiving. In a good holiday season, sales go up about 10 percent. This time, they went up 44 percent.

Everyone at Merry-Go-Round agrees on one thing: Harold is very good at business, and he should stick strictly to that. Especially, he should keep his nose out of anything resembling fashion.

Boogie's been on the road one time and tells Harold he needs a break. A sabbatical, he calls it. A slight vacation of maybe two months. While he's gone, he tells Harold, leave the other Merry-Go-Round buyers alone. Boogie's personally trained 16 of them. They might not have his precise instincts for fashion, but they're pretty good.

Harold nods his head, but his brain is clearly elsewhere. He figures, what's so tough about buying clothes? In fact, when he talks to close friends, he tends to disparage the whole clothing business. He calls it the rag business. He's much bigger than rags. He's getting closer to buying his own bank.

So, while Boogie's on sabbatical, Harold commences buying merchandise. When Boogie leaves town, Merry-Go-Round's got about $5 million in the company checking account. When he comes back, they owe that much.

What brings Boogie back to town is a phone call from Kenny Rodriguez, who's become their main buyer. Kenny tells Boogie, "If you want a business when you come back, you better come back now. Harold and Beth"—that's his new wife, for Rona's out of the picture by now—"have been going up to New York and doing the buying. And none of it's selling."

"He was burning up the cash," Boogie remembers. "He didn't know what he was doing. I come in, I've got fire in my eye. Harold's sitting there in his office. I'm steaming, and he sees it. And he kept a gun in his desk top drawer. He's afraid I'm gonna beat him up.

"So he pulls the gun out and says, 'Boogie, I'll shoot you, I'll shoot you.' I stopped right there. I said, 'Harold, get the fuck out of this building. I don't want to see you in this building, or I'll break your fuckin' head. You cost us millions in sales. Our buyers are petrified.' I got him out of the building and didn't let him in for nine months. He worked out of his home."

The gun incident's only the most dramatic sign of tension between the two. They're each capable of sarcasm straight out of diner days. When Boogie tells Harold he doesn't know what he's talking about, Harold snaps, "Oh, Boog, you're so deep."

After a while, he shortens the "deep" reference; he simply calls Boogie "Canyon."

They've got several hundred stores, and money pouring in, when they decide to go public. Annual sales are roughly $60 million. The initial stock offering is described as "fabulously successful." It nets Boogie and Harold about $13 million each. A secondary offering, a few years later, nets each another $16 million. By this time, they're each worth about $100 million, and still climbing.

What to do with all that money?

In Boogie's case, he's already begun spending plenty of it. Sometimes in big ways, sometimes not. He's got old pals who have fallen on rough times. Over lunch, he gives them a little money. Like $20,000 here, $30,000 there. One day, in line at Lenny's Deli, in suburban Owings Mills, he gets to talking to some stranger. Before they've ordered their sandwiches, Boogie's written the guy a four-figure check.

Early in the endless give-aways, his accountant warns him, "You can't give away this much. You gave away $800,000, but you only took home $300,000 this year."

Since the early Merry-Go-Round days, the Legg Mason firm has handled Boogie's finances. The portfolio was first handled by Jerry Scheinker and, for the past three decades, by his son Josh.

"Boogie wants to make as much money as he can," says Josh Scheinker in the summer of 2021, "because he wants to give away as much as he can. In an average day, I talk to him 10 to 15 times. We might talk three to four hours a day. Sometimes it's about the stock market, but it might be about the Orioles, or pro basketball.

"But lots of times he'll call and say, 'Wire this much money to this person.' I send out money four or five days a week. It'll be people from the old days, ex-girlfriends, people he was in a gang with, every single charity from Baltimore to Aspen. That's what he does. He doesn't want to be thanked or recognized. He just cares. It makes him feel good. He believes in karma. If he helps somebody, it adds years to his life.

"He's supported hundreds of people, hundreds. Friend of his from high school died broke, Boogie paid for the whole funeral. He just paid off an old friend's mortgage. In the last year, he's bought new cars for 18 different people. I'm literally wiring money to car dealers. The girl that cuts his wife's hair, he built a basketball court for her husband in their back yard. Random acts like the guy in line at Lenny's Deli.

"They're just standing there waiting for their sandwiches," says Scheinker, "and they're bullshitting a little. The guy's going through a rough time. I get a phone call at the office. It's Boogie. He's still standing in line with this guy. He says, 'Send this guy five grand.' That's just how he is."

When he lived at Hopkins House, he heard about an elderly woman named Flo who was having trouble paying her rent. Boogie barely knew her. He paid her rent every month until she died—a decade later.

"We're at Boogie's second wedding," says Baltimore sports journalist Stan (The Fan) Charles, an old friend, "and there's got to be 150 tables at the Woodholme Country Club. We're at a table with a woman who's got to be 85 years old. It was Flo. I ask her, 'How do you know Boogie?'

"She says, 'Oh, he's so wonderful.' She was being evicted from Hopkins House. Boogie happened to be coming through the lobby. He says, 'What's going on?' Within an hour or so, he made it clear he was paying her rent for the rest of her life."

Also, says Stan the Fan, she brought up Ralph Banner, Boogie's chauffeur and man-on-call, who's also co-best man at the wedding (along with Allan Charles, Stan's brother.)

"She says, 'Every couple of months, Ralph comes up and takes me to the racetrack and gives me $200 to play the horses.' Boogie's money, of course. I was at Hopkins House a lot," says Stan, "and Flo was at the main counter in the lobby all the time, like a piece of the furniture there. She was old and skinny and frail looking. How Boogie wound up taking a liking to her, I don't know."

You don't need to be a Freudian analyst to tie such an individual to Nettie Weinglass. Boogie moved his mother to nice digs in northwest Baltimore and took care of her every expense—and the full expenses of several of her closest friends, as well. She lived into her 90s.

"He moved his mother into a nice apartment on Ford's Lane, off Reisterstown Road," Allan Charles said. "He had a team of half a dozen women who would have been making $10 an hour any place else. Boogie paid them $30 an hour, maybe more, plus big bonuses. He said, 'They're gonna keep my mother alive. They don't want to lose this job. They know that when she dies, they go back to making $10 an hour with somebody else. You can bet they'll look after her.'"

Ron Matz, who spent half a century as a Baltimore news broadcaster, has known Boogie for the last four decades.

"I'm vacationing down in Naples, Fla., one time, where Boogie had a place," Matz said. "We're sitting on the beach, just me and Boogie. We're talking. Only the phone's ringing constantly. Every call is somebody who needs money. And every call, I hear him say, 'How much you need?' 'Ten thousand.' 'Okay, I'll send you the money.' Next guy, 'Twenty thousand.' 'Okay, I'll take care of it.'

"This kind of generosity. After all these calls, we're sitting there and he's giving all this money away, and he looks at me and says, 'Ronster, do you need any money?'

"He wants to be loved," says Matz. "Look, we all want to be loved. But he knows he's been so fortunate, he wants to help people. He's been so lucky to come from nothing and build an empire, and he wants to spread it around. But, to hear a guy on the phone, and Boogie says, 'It'll be in the bank tonight,' and you're sitting there and he tells you, 'I'm so glad I can help people…"

Matz's voice trails off at that thought. "There are a lot of people with money," he says, "who do nothing for others. He does it, and he does it quietly. And there are times I've asked him about specific people he's helped, and I have to stop because he breaks down talking about it."

Chapter Thirteen

"I Want to be a Boxer"

On February 5, 1977, Boogie and Harold find themselves at the Baltimore Civic Center. In its heyday, the place was home to the NBA Bullets basketball team with the fabulous Earl Monroe and Wes Unseld. It was home to a professional ice hockey team called the Baltimore Clippers. But, by this time, all are gone, including fans who once cheered them.

It takes a long time for Baltimoreans to venture downtown after dark in the extended aftermath of the '68 riots. Sports teams have fled, and so have department stores, and all those who once flocked to them.

But, on this night in 1977, the Civic Center is packed with boxing fans because something pretty dramatic in sports history has inexplicably arrived here. Sugar Ray Leonard, welterweight gold medal winner of the 1976 Olympics and arguably the biggest name in boxing once Muhammad Ali leaves the stage, has come here for his first professional bout.

He takes on a fellow called Luis Vega, misnamed The Bull to make him sound menacing. Leonard dispatches him in six rounds. The night is still young, and the 10,000 people in attendance hunger to see more punches thrown. So here come a couple of pugs who are clearly going nowhere.

"Look at this," Boogie tells Harold. "I could do better than this."

The two pugs are young guys with bulging muscles and ripped stomachs but no fighting skills perceivable to the naked eye. Or, at least, to Boogie's eye.

"They're throwing round-house punches," Boogie says. He's thinking about his street fighting days, and his combination punches, the right hand going straight in with the full power of the shoulder behind it.

"I could get in the ring right now, in street clothes, and beat either one of those guys," he tells Harold.

"You're full of shit," Harold replies. "Either one of them would kill you."

"Bet me," says Boogie.

"Twenty-five grand," says Harold.

"Make it fifty."

Such dollar amounts are beginning to feel small to them now. And so begins Boogie's newest adventure in making life more than a quest for more money than he'll ever be able to spend.

He is 36 years old, and he decides he'll become a professional boxer. When his mother hears this, she responds in the usual manner: "Label, you're a bissel meshugeh."

"*Leonard, you're a little crazy.*"

He's 20 years, minimum, past the age when young men decide to take up the sport in a serious manner. But he's filled with grandiosity and with the belief that his history of street fighting brings him all manner of useful experience.

To which we will briefly introduce the name Clem Florio. Clem's sitting a few seats away on the night of the Leonard-Vega fight, for he is a veteran boxing reporter (and horse racing handicapper) first for the Baltimore News American and then for the Washington Post.

Also, Clem's a retired professional boxer who tells a relatable story of his own beginnings in the sport. He grew up in Ozone Park, Queens, but found a gym somewhere in New Jersey where they wouldn't get picky over his age when he asked for a tryout.

The trainer there, some guy with a dented nose, asked, "You ever boxed before?"

"Sure," said Florio, approaching the truth at its margins. In retrospect, he recalled having beat up "a couple of sissies on the street" and, oh yeah, a junior high school gym teacher.

He trained for two days for his first match, a four-rounder that started badly. Florio was getting pounded. Between rounds, his corner man asked, "You ever fight before this?"

"No," Florio admitted.

"Any street fights?"

"Yeah."

"Well, get in there and street fight," the corner man said, "'cause you're getting killed."

Florio got shiners under both eyes, but he won the fight, which paid $25, though $13 went to his handlers.

But the point isn't money. It's street experience posing as boxing background to salvage the day—and it's pursuit of a dream. The difference is, Florio was 14 and lied about his age to break into the fight game. Boogie's 36, lying about his age for the same reason.

So he changes his entire lifestyle. He's going to bed early, he's skipping the club life, he's watching what he eats. He finds a gym over in East Baltimore where he decides he'll ask for a chance to become a real boxer.

He walks into the place wearing an old sleeveless basketball jersey, black shorts and sneakers. Some guy running the place asks what he wants. Boogie tells him.

"How old are you?" the guy says.

"Twenty-eight," Boogie says.

Then he hears a voice call out, "Hey, Boogie." It's an old friend, some guy who's hanging out at the gym. The guy's around Boogie's real age. So the trainer lets him box a round or two, but his cover's been blown. That's it, the trainer says, you're too old for us to be wasting time on you.

What now? He's serious about this thing. And he knows there's another gym, not far from here, where he might have a chance. It's Mack Lewis's gym, located at Broadway and Eager Street.

Mack's a legend in Baltimore. But the gym could be described, only with great charity, as a dump. It's a converted 19th century dance hall one creaky flight of stairs above street level. There are no showers, and no water at all. The place is heated only by a big wood-and coal-burning stove that Mack lights up each day. The boxers freeze in winter and swelter in summer. Everybody jokes that they should bottle the sunshine in the summer and store it in their lockers for winter. Money's so tight that there are boxers there who have to share mouth-pieces. But they manage to keep the gym going for half a century.

Mack Lewis grew up around East Baltimore's Patterson Park, one of a handful of black families in the neighborhood. He was a depression-era kid hustling for any edge. Sometimes he supplied bottles for the local bootleggers during Prohibition. Then he won a state Senate scholarship to the old Morgan State College, where he boxed and played both ways as a 170-pound football lineman.

The boxing stopped in the U.S. Army, where he suffered two busted eardrums in the ring. Discharged, he worked for the IRS for a long time and, with $1,000, he opened the old gym.

"It wasn't just the boxing," he said more than once. "It was the chance to work with kids who needed some help."

There were plenty of them. They lined up outside the gym and waited for the place to open. They dreamed of being another Sugar Ray Leonard or Muhammad Ali. Most of them, it was enough just to get them away from temptations of the streets and give them some discipline.

But, along the way, some world-class fighters came out of the gym and the training of Mack Lewis, including Hasim Rahman who briefly became heavyweight champion of the world, and Larry Middleton, who almost made it, and Vince Pettway, a future welterweight champ who will later declare his life was turned around—by Boogie Weinglass.

Alvin Anderson's another of the gym's immortals. He's a serious middleweight contender. And he's working out in the ring the night Boogie makes his first appearance there.

Boogie figures he's got to go in disguise. By this time, 1976, he's pretty well known in much of Baltimore—certainly, in much of middle class Baltimore—and he doesn't want to get chauffeured over in one of his limousines and walk in as some rich guy who's slumming.

He buys a 1956 Chevy for a couple of grand, and he beats up the car with a hammer to look like it's been through some rough times. He wants to look like a young working class guy.

The gym's located atop a package goods store, off an alley. He's got to climb 20 steps to get up there. He's slightly winded, and his heart's pounding, mostly from emotion, as he nears the top of the stairs and hears, as he recalls, "the speed bags chattering and the guys grunting as they're hitting the heavy bags, and you had to walk through these saloon doors."

And then, as he enters, there's complete silence, "like an E.F. Hutton commercial," he says all these years later. "You know, 'My broker's E.F. Hutton, and he says…' and then there's total silence so everybody in the commercial can hear. It's that kind of silence in the gym, because you never, ever see some white guy come in. Me, it didn't bother, and never did. I had a black girlfriend in high school. I played basketball with a lot of black guys. I lived in mixed neighborhoods."

But he knows this is still an edgy hour in the post-riot history of race in Baltimore. And he remembers Alvin Anderson, in the midst of sparring, stop and lean over the ropes to stare at him. Guys who were jumping rope suddenly stop. Nobody's hitting the speed bags. And Mack Lewis, sitting in a chair, gets up and walks over to Boogie.

"Son, can I help you?" he asks.

"Yes, sir, I'd like to box."

"What do you mean?" It's as if such words simply don't compute, not in this time, not in this place.

"I want to box."

"Have you ever boxed before?

"Yes, sir. In New York."

"What's your name?"

"Lenny Wine," says Boogie. Then he spells it out, so Mack doesn't think it's "Wein" and attaches "glass" to it to connect him to Merry-Go-Round and money.

Mack gives him a hearty slap on his shoulder. "Well, you got good shoulders," he says. Alvin Anderson's still staring from the ring, wondering what this idiot white boy's doing here. "But I never heard of you."

"I only fought amateur," says Boogie. "Eight or nine fights. Never got beat."

"Where do you work? Everybody in here works days."

"I'm unemployed right now."

Mack calls over a young fighter named Leroy to show Boogie around the gym. Mack's got another fighter he's working with. Leroy's showing "Wine" around when another fighter comes by and shoves Boogie aside with his shoulder. It's a kind of test. Boogie instinctively throws a left into the guy, and then a right, and then they're both on the floor fighting like mad.

A bunch of boxers gathers around them. Mack pulls them apart. Leroy tells him, "Mr. Mack, I saw what happened. Wine didn't do nothing."

Mack turns to the other fighter. "Get out of the gym right now," he says.

As the guy's escorted out, Mack tells Boogie, "I'm embarrassed. You come back tomorrow, and we'll put you in the ring."

When he shows up the next evening, he finds Mack Lewis smiling. "Wine, nobody thought you'd come back," he says.

"I'm serious about this," Boogie tells him. "Just give me time to get in shape."

So he's doing sit-ups, jumping rope, hitting the heavy bag, getting himself pretty exhausted on that second night, when a fellow comes up and tells Boogie, "Mr. Mack says he wants to see what you got."

When Boogie looks his way, he sees Mack holding up a pair of boxing gloves. He thinks: Already? So he tells Mack, "I'm tired, I've been working out all evening."

"Don't worry about it," Mack says. "I just want to see you move." He points to the ring, where he wants Boogie to spar with Alvin Anderson, who's been staring balefully at Boogie since yesterday. He's the 5th ranked middleweight in the world and about a dozen pounds heavier than Boogie.

"And don't throw your right hand," Mack tells him.

They're about 30 seconds into the first round, and Boogie's a little hyper, ducking and dancing, and he hears Mack out of a corner tell him, "Wine, calm down. Move and stick, move and stick."

So he gets through it all right. Second round, Anderson ties him into a corner and won't let him out. Instinct overcomes instruction. Boogie throws a right hand into Anderson's nose, which draws blood. Anderson is not pleased.

"He comes after me," Boogie says, "and I'm hoping like hell for the bell to ring, and I heard the worst words I heard in my whole life. It's Mack, and he says, 'Alvin, turn up the heat a little bit.'"

Alvin drops him with a right hand in the stomach.

"I told you not to throw the right," Boogie hears Mack say.

He learns to take advice. It's not something that comes naturally to this man, 36 years old, who's come here from the comforts of unanticipated wealth, and all-night partying, to get knocked around by a bunch of tough-ass strangers half his age.

But he sticks with it, and he makes it work for several months, not only for himself but for the whole Mack Lewis troupe. For now a remarkable run of good fortune begins to play itself out, which commences at the start of an evening when Mack gathers the whole gang, 30 or 40 fighters, for the gentle evening benediction before they start beating each other's brains out.

"Lord," Mack intones, as the boxers link hands in front of him, "please let my boxers hone their skills so they can make a living at it. And please let them escape serious injury. And, lord, please bless the angel who is sending us money."

For now there begins a run of anonymous checks arriving at the gym, made out to "Mack Lewis Gymnasium," sent over naturally by Boogie's financial people.

The checks usually go for about $1,000, but they're only a piece of the good fortune. Also arriving are new boxing gloves, new heavy bags, new mouthpieces. Sometimes a note will come with the checks: "Buy something for the kids," the notes say.

And then, one day, comes a brand new station wagon, which seats 10 people, so that, for the first time, none of Mack Lewis's fighters will ever have to worry how they'll get to the next evening's road trips when a bunch of them share the same card.

All of this given, quite anonymously, by Lenny Wine.

"He never suspected me," Boogie reflects decades later. "Not with me showing up every day in that '56 Chevy." But Mack must have had some notions, especially when the whole troupe would stop somewhere after an evening's road trip to get something to eat, and this Lenny Wine fellow would say, "I got this," whenever the check arrived.

Among the other gym regulars is a kid just approaching his teens. It's Vincent Pettway, the world's future welterweight champion. He started boxing when he was eight.

Years later, he remembers watching Boogie sparring. "He had some ability," Pettway recalls. 'He had some real skills. I can't tell you if he could punch or not, but he was fluid. He sparred with some very tough guys. You had to be able to hold your own to get in there, and then to come back again. And he did."

He did more than that. He spotted Pettway as a serious young guy who needed a couple of breaks. When Pettway reached adolescence, Boogie gave him a job at Merry-Go-Round, and when he needed a way to travel, Boogie bought him a car to get around.

"He wanted to make sure I got to work, and got to the gym," says Pettway, who later retired from the ring and went to work for the city of Baltimore's Department of Public Works.

"He took me off the street. He was a guy that believed in my ability to get ahead. He changed my life, no other way to say it. And never asked for nothing, and never made himself out to be some big shot. If you didn't know who he was, you wouldn't believe who he was."

He was one more thing: the gym's savior. When the building was in danger of being sold to a grocer, Boogie guaranteed payment for a 10-year lease.

"I just saw what Mack was doing for so many kids," Boogie said, "without reaping any financial reward. I figured somebody ought to be lending more than just moral support."

Chapter Fourteen

And Starring as Boogie is... Boogie!

The boxing goes away, but other signs of restlessness do not. There's always Hollywood he could conquer. In 1981, Barry Levinson tells Boogie he's about to make a movie, called "Diner," about coming of age in Baltimore in the late '50s. It's based on their era, and their gang. He says there's a character in the movie named Boogie. Barry and Boogie have a little chat about casting. What about Boogie himself playing Boogie?

He was pushing 40 now. The movie Boogie was half that age, but the real Boogie was still in great shape from boxing. They talked about putting makeup on Boogie's face to make him look 20 again. The conversation was somewhere between serious casting and amiable kibitzing, until Levinson mentioned early-morning shooting schedules. And that was the end of all of this crazy movie star talk.

"He said I'd have to be on the set at 6:30 in the morning," Boogie recalled, "and I said, 'I don't come *in* until 6:30.' So that was that. But I could have done it. I could play myself, I could be Boogie. Boogie playing Boogie, how tough would that be?"

When that didn't work out, Levinson asked Boogie to interview several actors who might be the right movie Boogie. Levinson interviewed hundreds of actors—he estimates about 500—to get the right starring cast. Mickey Rourke was everybody's choice to be Boogie.

"Rourke fell in love with the fact that I'd been boxing," Boogie said. "He tried it later. He couldn't box like me. But he was a street guy like me."

Of course, the streets were a little different from real life to the movies. The movie was shot in Baltimore. But the real Hilltop Diner was gone by 1981, so they found an old look-alike diner somewhere in New Jersey and transplanted it down to Boston Street, along Southeast Baltimore's waterfront.

Boogie stayed away from the shooting. He didn't want to impose. Allan Charles told him, "Man, you gotta go down to the set. This is a movie about you."

Three in the morning, Charles and Boogie show up on Boston Street, at the movie diner, in a white stretch limo with "BOOG" on the license plates. There's a break in the all-night shooting.

"How's my movie going?" Boogie says when he sees Levinson. Then the two Boogies, real and pretend, greet each other like old friends.

"Rourke idolized me a little bit," Boogie says now.

He certainly liked the jeans Boogie was wearing, and said so. The jeans were straight out of Merry-Go-Round stock.

"Here," Boogie tells Rourke, "try 'em on."

And, with much of the cast and crew and neighborhood bystanders looking on, Boogie immediately drops his pants. He's standing there, three in the morning on Boston Street, in his bikini briefs. He hands over his jeans to Rourke, who's laughing out loud.

"He liked my pants and I liked his," says Boogie. "We were about the same size. I think we wound up switching pants."

It was a sweet moment during a convivial six-week shoot. These were break-through movie roles for those such as Ellen Barkin, Kevin Bacon, Steve Guttenberg, Tim Daly, Paul Reiser, Daniel Stern and Rourke.

Also, it was Levinson's rookie job as director. He's still figuring things out on the first day, when they do their first shot. It's a pool room. Is it based on Benny's or Knocko's from the old days? Who knows? Levinson knew both places, though he tended toward Knocko's, and not just because it was closer to his Forest Park neighborhood.

"You had to be 14 or so to get into Knocko's," Levinson remembers. "Knocko was a great character, but the big thing we liked, he'd allow us to have an account. 'I got a coke here, put it on my account.' Or, 'I got some M&M's. Put it on my account.'"

Anyway, first day of shooting, first scene and it's in this poolroom. The actors are nervous. Levinson's not saying anything. And a guy with a clapper hollers, "Rolling. Take One. Mark it. Speed, and…"

And there's a silence, and everybody's waiting. Nobody moves, nobody says anything. And finally there's a whisper, as an assistant director leans over and says to Levinson, "Uh, you have to say 'Action.'"

Oh. "Action," says Levinson.

Everybody cracks up. It's a nice start—to a directing career, and a way of telling stories. Three decades down the road, Vanity Fair Magazine will run a cover story calling "Diner," "The Most Influential Movie of the Last 30 Years."

The veteran film critic Michael Sragow will write, "(Diner) crystallized the 'observational' humor that would dominate

American comedy for decades, whether in TV series like 'Seinfeld,' Larry David's 'Curb Your Enthusiasm,' or Judd Apatow's stream of big-screen hits."

It wasn't just reaching for the joke, it was guys shooting the bull and things happening based on character. And who was a bigger character than Boogie?

On the night of the "Diner" premiere at Baltimore's Senator Theater, Boogie arrives on dressed-up York Road in his chauffeur-driven Rolls Royce, for which he paid $125,000 in cash. He's got new girlfriend Pepper beside him in an impossibly short miniskirt that he insisted upon. His chauffeur opens the door, and out pops Boogie, in jeans and cowboy boots and a tee shirt that says, "Original Diner Guy."

Watching the movie that night, he recalls, "was surreal. Only thing, I probably could have played myself. But after that, wherever I went, people heard 'Boogie' and they knew me. I was sort of popular before that, but it was for fighting, or basketball, or for stealing a police car. This was definitely bigger."

So he was bigger now, and richer, too. What do you do with all that money? How about buying a major league baseball team, or maybe a pro football franchise? How about buying a couple of new homes? Those are signs of the truly rich, and he's already got some of the other symbols.

A couple of limousines, for example, and that classy Rolls Royce which once belonged to some descendant of Eli Whitney, inventor of the cotton gin. And what's a luxury limo without a chauffeur behind the wheel?

The chauffeur is Ralph Banner, a six-foot, 325-pound pal who does extra duty as Boogie's cook, penthouse mate, best friend, bodyguard and, eventually, co-best man at Boogie's second wedding. Ralph stays with Boogie, until his death.

He was living in North Carolina, sometimes working as a short-order cook, and sometimes laboring in a cotton field there, when somebody showed him a newspaper ad reading, "Wanted: Cook/driver for wealthy gentleman." Ralph responded to the ad. Boogie responded to Ralph. They clicked right away. Ralph was a big, happy, unsophisticated guy who dug Boogie's open-arms approach to life right away.

"He loved me, and I loved him," Boogie said.

In pop culture, says Allan Charles, who did Merry-Go-Round's TV commercials and shared best-man honors at Boogie's second wedding, "the closest thing to Ralph is like Leon from Larry David's 'Curb Your Enthusiasm.' Boogie didn't treat him as his guy Friday, or his man servant. He was his equal. He became a celebrity. I used him in a lot of commercials. The lottery, Parks Sausages. But he became one of the guys. If we went in to get a bite at 3 in the morning at Sabatino's, Ralph didn't wait out in the car. He came in and ate with us. One of the guys."

"He had a couple of girlfriends," Boogie said, "but if I needed him, he left. I'd call him at 2 in the morning to pick up a date. I'd go down to Little Italy with a bunch of pals, and he became one of the guys. And he'd chauffeur my mother and her friends."

That's when Nettie would ask Boogie, "Label, would you send the station vagon around?"

But one time the station wagon—the limousine—was unavailable. "In the shop, mom," Boogie explained, "but I'll send Ralph around with another car."

Ralph could drive the BMW Boogie bought for him, but the BMW's being repaired. So he takes Boogie's '56 Thunderbird convertible. Two front seats, and that's all. When he gets to Nettie's place, she's thrown him a curve. She's got two other elderly Jewish ladies with her. Like Nettie, they're past 80, and they want to go to the Rogers Avenue Synagogue.

This will take some maneuvering, three old women and a very large man jammed into two small seats. The Thunderbird seems even smaller now, owing at least partly to Ralph's 325 pounds. His right hip extends past the car's midsection. He takes down the top of the convertible so everyone can try to squeeze in. One of the elderly ladies will have to sit on the other elderly lady's lap. And Nettie? She'll sit on Ralph's lap while he attempts to drive.

The ladies are miffed right away, since their hair's getting messed up in the wind. Ralph's having some trouble moving between the gas pedal and the brake while negotiating the gear shift. He's so large, Nettie's head's sticking above the windshield, and Ralph's having trouble seeing the road. The ladies are all holding on to their hair as the four of them head toward the synagogue with people all along crowded Reisterstown Road gawking at the sight.

Naturally, they get pulled over. The cop who stops them says, "What the hell's going on here?" He asks this in a tone that implies, "Ladies, is this large black man attempting to kidnap you in someone's stolen car?"

"This is Mr. Weinglass's car, sir," Ralph quickly explains. "I'm his driver. He owns the Merry-Go-Round clothing outlets." Just to make sure the cop believes him, Ralph starts listing every single Merry-Go-Round location in the greater Baltimore metropolitan area.

"Yes, my son Label," Nettie chimes in. "Merry-Go-Round."

"Where are you going?"

"Rogers Avenue Synagogue," Ralph says.

"Follow me," says the cop.

They get a police escort to the synagogue, complete with flashing light. As the ladies exit, the cop tells Ralph, "Sir, you can't do that any more. No heads above the windshield. And don't forget seat belts."

Ralph's on board for the scary times, as well.

One night, they're coming home from an Orioles game in Boogie's limo. Four wise-ass guys start tailgating and beeping their horn when they see this big black guy driving a fancy car. This offends these geniuses. When they hit a red light just outside Hopkins House where Boogie and Ralph live, Boogie jumps out of the limo, walks back to the horn honkers, and asks if there's a problem. One of them, the driver, rolls down the window and points a gun at Boogie's head.

"What's it to you, Jewboy?" he says.

Boogie's standing there, utterly frozen, but he's thinking about dropping down and running to the back of the car. But here comes Ralph. He snatches Boogie like a twig and stands between him and the gunman. Then he locks eyes with this moron.

He tells him, "Boy, you better put that car in reverse or pull that trigger."

Boogie's ducking behind Ralph, wondering if the bullet will go through Ralph and kill both of them. Then comes a screeching of tires. The driver's put his car in reverse, floored the pedal—and driven right into the brick entrance to the Hopkins House apartments. The back end of the car's bashed in, the fender's stuck to a tire, and the lady at the front desk of Hopkins House has seen the whole thing and called the police, who arrive moments later to take away the four guys with the gun.

Take note here that Boogie and Ralph were returning from an Orioles baseball game when all of this occurred. Across the years, Boogie's passion for sports burns so brightly that it nearly results in major league ownership.

There comes a time when the Baltimore Orioles are available. In this era, the Orioles may be the classiest organization in all of baseball. They've just played in their fourth World Series in the last dozen years. They've bid farewell to the Hall of Famers Brooks and Frank Robinson, but they've still got Jim Palmer and Eddie Murray, and young Cal Ripken's on the way. Over a 20-year period, from 1965 to 1985, the Orioles win more games than any other team in major league baseball.

But they find themselves, in 1979, for sale. The owner is Jerold Hoffberger, whose family wishes to cash in. Oh, if they only knew a few things about money and baseball. In 1993, the Orioles will be sold once more—for $173 million. In 2021, their estimated value is $1.4 billion.

But, in 1979, Jerry Hoffberger is asking only $12 million to buy arguably the classiest team in all of professional sports.

"Let's buy the Orioles," says Harold.

"Sure," says Boogie. The reality of this is not quite kicking in yet. "I could make my brother Jackie the third base coach. He needs a job. And maybe let Ralph coach first base."

He's joking. But, the more they talk about it, the more the idea feels real. So Harold calls Hoffberger's office and sets up an appointment. Then he calls Boogie. This could be a marriage made in heaven, with these two home-town guys swimming in money and passionate from birth about Baltimore sports teams.

And yet, the timing is not so smart, since Harold makes the most crucial phone call to Boogie at 8 in the morning. Harold's been up for a while, naturally, having slept through the night with his wife and growing family. But Boogie's just getting in from his normal night of partying.

"Don't forget," says Harold, "we've got our meeting with Hoffberger today."

"Right," says Boogie. "I'll be there."

"I think things are looking good," says Harold. No other local people have expressed interest in buying the club. "So don't screw it up by saying something outlandish."

"Fuck you," says Boogie. This is standard give-and-take between these two, until the very next sentence.

"And put on a coat and tie," says Harold.

"What do you mean?" says Boogie.

"Coat and tie," says Harold. "You can't do a deal like this in jeans and sneakers. Put on a suit."

"Forget it. No suit. I don't even own a suit."

"You can't go and embarrass me," says Goldsmith.

"Then I ain't going," says Weinglass, holding on to his inner Boogie.

And so he doesn't go, nor does a ticked-off Harold, and thus are the Baltimore Orioles sold to Edward Bennett Williams, the world-famous attorney out of Washington, D.C.

"They had a deal to buy the Orioles," recalls one of Boogie's long-time attorneys, Ray Altman. "They had a meeting set up, and Boogie refused to go. The price was $12 million. Boogie didn't care about the money. He pictured himself taking a few at-bats. That's how he thinks. But it was a matter of principle. He probably could have put on a sports jacket and a string tie, but he wasn't gonna do it. He would have been the man. That's how he lived. But he's real sorry he didn't wear that coat and tie."

Goodbye Orioles, and goodbye to a vanishing era of Baltimore home-town money bankrolling Baltimore sports franchises.

And hello to a time of extended nervousness about professional sports in Baltimore.

Already, the town has lost its professional basketball franchise, the Baltimore Bullets. They were wonderful for about a decade, when Wes Unseld and Gus Johnson were setting off fast breaks to Earl Monroe and downtown's Civic Center was packed with roaring crowds.

But, in the aftermath of the '68 riots, the crowds only showed up sporadically. The team's owner was Abe Pollin. In a lot of cities, local owners rode out the post-riot anxiety and waited for the day when downtown could be rediscovered. But, in Baltimore, the out-of-town owner Pollin looked at the red ink in his ledgers and, in 1973, transferred the Bullets to Largo, in the wealthy Montgomery County suburbs of Washington, D.C.

Then came the '79 sale of the Orioles to Edward Bennett Williams, the ultimate Washington legal and political insider. Williams was asked if he intended to keep the team in Baltimore or move them 40 miles south to D.C.

A ridiculous question, of course. Who would even dream of moving the classiest team in sports, the winningest team in baseball fresh off a World Series appearance, from its historic home?

"No," Williams says, he will not move the team, "as long as there's adequate fan support."

But he refuses to say what "adequate" means. It's the only ransom note in history without a specific price tag. Williams refuses to define the term over the next decade as more than 20 million people trek into Memorial Stadium to watch the Orioles play sometimes glorious and sometimes tragicomic baseball, which will include a 1988 season in which they open with 21 consecutive losses.

Never in history had so awful a team gotten so much support for so little reason.

Yet, because of Williams' ties to Washington, and because of his oblique language, the gun was never removed from Baltimore sports fans' heads.

And then the gun was cocked.

By the winter of 1983, the Orioles were still golden, but the beloved football Colts were not. The Colts were Baltimore's secular religion, and Memorial Stadium its outdoor cathedral. In '83, the Orioles had just beaten the Philadelphia Phillies in the World Series—but the Colts were awful.

The glad Sunday afternoons of John Unitas throwing to Raymond Berry and Lenny Moore were over, and the midnight threats of Robert Irsay had arrived. The longtime owner of the Colts, Carroll Rosenbloom, sold the team to Irsay, an air conditioning magnate from Chicago. He proceeded to dismantle the team and ruin all historic fan loyalty.

And then he stole the team out of Baltimore in the middle of one snowy night in March, 1984, and took them all the way to Indianapolis.

No NFL football in Baltimore, and no NBA basketball. And now, as Edward Bennett Williams succumbed to cancer, his estate sold the team in December, 1988, to another out-of-town owner, a financier and attorney from New York, Eli Jacobs. The price was now $70 million, plus assumption of another $17 million in deferred player salaries and other debts.

But Jacobs was discovered, after only a few years, to be in over his head. Drowning in debt, he looked to sell the team. For Baltimoreans, this raised every insecurity in their repertoire. Would local investors step forward, or would the club go to some out-of-town shark who would move them? Would any local investor be able to afford the new asking price, which would now reach $173 million, a long way from Jerry Hoffberger's $12 million?

Into the fray comes Boogie, and this time he might even put on a coat and tie.

The newspapers and broadcast stations make him an instant player. On his sports radio talk show, Stan (The Fan) Charles reveals that Boogie wants to buy the team, and he's got other people with local ties who want to pitch in.

There's Barry Levinson, who's just made his third movie, "Avalon," about life in the beloved Baltimore of his youth. There's Tom Clancy, the best-seller author who's also from Baltimore. And there's Baltimorean Peter Angelos, the attorney who's made a fortune in asbestos lawsuits.

Boogie's serious, but still making jokes about it. "I've got my three kids," he says, "so maybe I'd make my son Bo a scout. Give him something to do. Sage could do PR. I'm not gonna be another Steinbrenner"—meaning George Steinbrenner, the tyrannical owner of the New York Yankees. "The idea is to have fun."

The newspapers say Boogie's worth more than $100 million at this point. He has more than 600 stores around the country under seven different names. He immediately declares that, whatever millions he might spend for the team, he'd quickly spend millions more to purchase top flight free agents to make the team a winner.

"This isn't about money," Boogie tells reporters. "This is more emotional than financial. If it was strictly business, I wouldn't even consider it. I'd do better keeping my money in the bank. The return's better, and it's a lot less stress."

The wheeling and dealing stretches across the summer of 1991, as Eli Jacobs clings to ownership despite his financial world's hidden troubles. Finally there's a face-to-face meeting in a fancy law office, Boogie and Jacobs, along with a mediator.

Boogie looks at Jacobs and immediately thinks he's never seen anyone so uptight. The guy looks like he's somebody on a last march along Death Row. Nobody yet knows how much financial trouble Jacobs has. He starts out asking for $150 million for the team.

"Way too much," Boogie tells him. "TV revenues are down, salaries are up."

Jacobs mentions big-money friends of his. He sounds like a snob. He mentions his background at Harvard and Yale. He wants to show Boogie that he knows very important people.

"Eli," he tells him, after about 15 minutes, "why don't you fuckin' loosen up?"

The meeting lasts about 90 minutes, but nothing gets settled. Boogie walks out feeling Jacobs is a lost soul.

Jacobs had one glorious moment that summer. Elizabeth, queen of England, came to America and decided to take in a baseball game. She sat in the owner's box at Memorial Stadium with Jacobs.

At that moment, Boogie was vacationing at one of several homes he now owned. This one was in Ocean City, Md. A reporter reached him there, and asked what it might have been like to meet the queen.

"It would have been beautiful," he said, relaxing on the beach and presumably building sand castles in the air. "I'd have been cordial and nice, but I'd be me. For the queen, I'd have worn my boots or my tennis shoes. Hey, I don't own anything but boots and tennis shoes."

Well, he didn't get the team after all, but other local interests did. Peter Angelos signed on as majority owner, and Levinson and Clancy bought into minority pieces. But a deal for a different ballclub was just around the corner, and this one touched Boogie's heart—and Baltimore's—in the most intimate way.

Chapter Fifteen

"Give Boogie the Ball"

In his rapturous youth, there were two religions woven into Boogie's life: Judaism, and the Baltimore Colts. It was this way for an entire generation of Baltimoreans, no matter which God in heaven they worshipped.

The Colts were an emblem of municipal pride for a city with a historic inferiority complex. Without the Colts, Baltimore saw itself as a wayward third cousin stuck along a railroad track somewhere between the glamorous New York and the political power of Washington, D.C.

But the Colts gave Baltimore bragging rights.

New York had the Yankees and football Giants, and Wall Street and Broadway. But Baltimore had the Colts' championship game triumph of 1958—dubbed "the greatest game ever played" - that forever changed America's dominant sports culture from baseball to pro football.

Washington had Dwight Eisenhower, but the Colts had John Unitas. The nation's capitol had congress, called the world's finest deliberative body. But Baltimore had Memorial Stadium, called the world's largest outdoor insane asylum.

It gave the whole town a rollicking tribal identity. You had to be there on Sunday afternoons, to be part of it, even if you didn't have a ticket. Naturally, Boogie didn't have one. At the Hilltop Diner back then, the guys chattered into the early morning hours plotting scams to sneak into the ballpark.

One fellow knew the stadium guard who let the supply trucks in. For fifteen bucks, he'd let eight or nine guys sneak in with the trucks. Some Sundays, Boogie and his pal Jan Abrams would hitch-hike to the park. They had maybe $2 in their pockets, and raw chutzpah.

"There was a special entrance for the band," Abrams said, "and sometimes we'd walk in with them. We'd wait for the guys with the biggest instruments. 'Here, let me carry that for you.' Just walk in, and walk around until the game started.

"Or there were two aisles of ticket takers, and you could slip between them, holding up our hands like we've got tickets, and then run through. They couldn't run after us, because they're still collecting tickets.

"Plus, there were wires on the side of the stadium, going up to the ramps between the upper and lower decks. We took this guy Yussel with us. Boogie and I climbed the wire in 10 or 15 seconds, but Yussel couldn't make it. The cops found him when he was halfway up. But you found some way in, because you had to be there. You had to."

When Barry Levinson made "Diner," the comic highlight of the movie was the guy who won't marry unless his fiancée passes a written test about the Colts. Everybody in America thought this was quite outrageous, except people in Baltimore, for whom the premise made perfect sense. Who could marry somebody who didn't love the Colts?

Some years later, attorney Donald Saiontz, one of the original diner gang, said there were actually "a bunch of guys" who gave their girlfriends such tests.

"Why would that be unusual?" Saiontz asked, his expression absolutely deadpan. "I'm not saying guys wouldn't get married if a girl didn't care about the Colts. But how could you hang with a girl who didn't care?"

What the baseball Dodgers had been to Brooklyn before they fled to the west coast, the football Colts were to Baltimore. Their midnight run to Indianapolis took the heart out of an entire metro area, which begged and plotted for a replacement team while mourning the loss of the Colts over the next decade.

And so the ruling class of the NFL decided to toy with Baltimore. In the summer of 1992, eight years after the Colts' kidnapping, the league announced that two cities would get new franchises.

If Baltimore wanted an expansion team, they'd need people with deep pockets to step forward—and they'd need the whole town to show its enduring love for the game. They'd have to start this process by filling Memorial Stadium for a meaningless mid-summer exhibition contest between two teams, Miami and New Orleans, about whom absolutely no one in Baltimore cared even slightly.

The town responded, and so did Boogie—and then the town responded to Boogie.

At NFL headquarters in New York, he forked over $100,000 for the right to be considered as owner of a team here—if Baltimore should, in fact, get a team.

He was up against Malcolm Glazer, a wealthy real estate man. Glazer was from Florida. His pockets were so deep that some idiot writer at the Baltimore Sun, who apparently slept through the ownership troubles with out-of-towners Robert

Irsay, Edward Bennett Williams, Eli Jacobs and Abe Pollin, wrote an editorial headlined: "NFL Expansion: Cash Counts."

It was a naked plug for Glazer. It read, in part: "Mr. Glazer has the financial wherewithal and the willingness to buy a team for Baltimore even if it costs $200 million in cash…This is the kind of financial clout that would put Baltimore back in contention for a professional football team."

From my desk at The Sun, where I was writing a column three times a week, I telephoned Weinglass, who was living part of the year in Aspen, Colorado, when he wasn't living in Baltimore or in Ocean City, Md.

All that constrained him from throwing a punch, he said, was the fact that he was 2,000 miles from whoever wrote such an editorial.

"How about this?" he said. "I've put a group together, and it's all Baltimore guys. And we've got at least as much money as Glazer, and probably more. He can write a check for the whole amount, and so can we. I keep hearing how wealthy this Glazer is. Does anybody know that, between me and Bernstein alone"—that was David Bernstein, chairman of the board of Duty Free International—"the market capitalization of our businesses is one billion, five hundred million dollars? And it's Baltimore-based money."

"One-point-five billion?" I asked.

"Yeah, but don't write it that way. Write it so it sounds like something: one billion, five hundred million. And money isn't even the point here."

Robert Irsay had no heart for Baltimore, and so he took the Colts west. Edward Bennett Williams sensed the emotional vulnerability of the town and made sure everyone knew he could move away at any time. Abe Pollin took off in an era when a wounded Baltimore was recovering from riots.

"To me," Boogie said, local ownership was the key. "Everybody in my group's a true Baltimorean. This is where our hearts are. Look, I could have bought franchises in other cities. I've had the offers, but I wouldn't even consider it. If it's not Baltimore, it's not gonna happen for me."

And then he started mentioning names—not those business people in his ownership group, but those Baltimore Colts in his memory. He pulled out names from decades earlier: Buddy Young and Bert Rechichar, Gino Marchetti and Lenny Moore, and a corner of the end zone called Orrsville.

"Every time I hear the words Colts on TV now, and it's Indianapolis they're talking about, I can't even watch it," he said. "Every time I see that horseshoe on the helmet, I get sick. And it could happen again. Look, I can understand another ownership group beating me out, if they're able. But for any outside group, Malcolm Glazer or anybody, that would be a tragedy for Baltimore."

The town took his words to heart. The TV and radio stations played up the local ownership angle, and fans understood the need to fill Memorial Stadium for the meaningless Miami-New Orleans exhibition.

At four o'clock on a frigid January morning, a full day before tickets would go on sale for the following summer's contest, the line began to form at Memorial Stadium. One guy pitched a tent to stay warm. Others began throwing a football around. By dawn's early light, scores of fans were waiting for tickets, whose sale was still a day away.

The next day, the game sold out completely in a couple of hours. In the months to follow, Boogie and his partners—business people mostly, but Barry Levinson, as well—met with NFL officials to discuss sale details, should Baltimore get an expansion team.

"I'm not looking to buy a ballclub to make money," Boogie said. "What am I gonna do, be like one of these suits who die with all their money in the bank, these guys with a hundred million dollars who get on the phone Monday mornings and start screaming at people so they can make another $5 million. What for? A hundred percent of this is about fun, and that's all. I'm Boogie. I'm not gonna change."

We met for brunch one Sunday that winter, at the Suburban House Restaurant on Reisterstown Road. He eyed a TV screen, where two teams played in a game holding no interest for Baltimore fans.

"Look at that," somebody hollered. "Even the cheerleaders are awful."

"Yeah," somebody else called to him, "when you get us a team, Boog, you gotta get a dozen of the best looking cheerleaders in the world."

"Nah," he said.

"No cheerleaders?"

"Not a dozen," Boogie said. He swept his hand across the room. "We're gonna have 300 cheerleaders, and they're gonna cover that whooole field."

And yet, as Barry Levinson remembered years later, "We were very serious about it. We went to Chicago a couple of times to meet with NFL people. Boogie was real serious. He had all kinds of ideas."

Then came the muggy night, in August of 1992, when 60,000 fans filled Memorial Stadium for that meaningless pre-season exhibition game.

"What I remember," said Levinson, "is driving down to the stadium that evening with Boogie. And then walking around the field before the game, and the fans are yelling, 'Boogie, Boogie.' I got such a kick out of it."

It wasn't just the moment that pleased him, but the memory of so much that preceded it. Levinson thought about the aimless kid he knew years earlier, hungry to be accepted, now hearing people chanting his name. As Boogie listened, a look of sheer delight passed across his face.

He went with Levinson into the Miami Dolphins locker room for a few minutes. Equipment managers were arranging uniforms for the game, and here were these two vastly wealthy men, giddy in the presence of those who arrange shoulder pads for a living.

Life has to be more than money, Boogie insisted. They remembered watching the Colts of three decades earlier, and they needled each other. It sounded vaguely like knock sessions from the diner of 30 years earlier.

"I don't want to say Barry was rich," Boogie said, "but his family had tickets. I had to climb over the fence in back of left field and sneak in through that tunnel back there. I was in high school then."

"High school?" said Levinson. "This is a guy who graduated high school at 20. We figured he was getting his doctorate in high school."

I sat with the two of them in Section 32 of Memorial Stadium's upper deck that night. The game was a stinker, but most people weren't watching, anyway. The fans knew their role in this game. They were there strictly as props to impress the NFL money guys. Sixty thousand people hoped they weren't being played for suckers.

"All these people who made the Colts their lives," Boogie said, as his eyes swept across the big stadium crowd. "I get choked up thinking about it. There'll never be another city like Baltimore."

Levinson nodded his head and gestured toward the old Colts band, still wearing their faded blue and white uniforms.

"That band," he said, voice full of wonder. "What other town has a band with no team? The team's gone, but the band's still playing. It takes your breath away."

The two men went back to a sweeter time, which they wanted to recreate. But now their words were swallowed by another sound, which came from great swaths of the big crowd, a chant that sounded like some vast political chorus.

"Give Boogie the ball," they roared. "Give Boogie the ball."

Boogie sat silently for a few minutes, taking it in, and then he leaned over and said softly, "You know, I had a real inferiority complex for a lot of years."

"How about right now?" I asked.

"This helps," he said, smiling slightly.

But the NFL helped not at all. The league turned its back on Baltimore and gave expansion franchises to two other cities. The exhibition game meant nothing, the overflow crowd meant nothing, and neither did Baltimore's proud football history.

"You know," Boogie said later, "I grew up on Baker Street, and guys did a lot of things to stay alive. It was tough down there. But I'll tell you, there was more honesty in that neighborhood than in this whole NFL process."

Chapter Sixteen

Million Dollar Gambles

He was married now. He met Pepper in 1981, married her a few years later, raised three children with her and stayed married for the next two decades. As Merry-Go-Round flourished, he invented a place called Boogie's Diner, which took on a life of its own. And, through it all, he kept spending his money, one way or another.

He gave it to hard-luck friends, and to strangers, too. He gave it away on whims. He gave it to the card tables in Las Vegas, and the bookmakers who took his insane sports bets. And he survived all of it and moved on.

Life had to be about more than money. Those humorless country club millionaires, who didn't know how to enjoy themselves despite their riches, taught him that much. And he understood that life was brief. His father's death taught him that. And so did the death of Eggy.

His father was dying for years, going back to those smoky card games when the family lived down on Baker Street. But Eggy's was a blind-side hit. He was 36. On the surface, he was doing all right. He'd moved from managing the Towson Merry-Go- Round to running the whole chain's allocations.

When merchandise came into the warehouse, it was Eggy who handled which stores got which goods.

But he'd never gotten past his father's DNA. The money came in, and he gambled it back out. He lost $40,000 in a day. When Eggy couldn't cover the bets, the bookies leaned on Boogie, who bailed him out more than once.

But the big losses kept coming. One night, pressured by some strong-arm types, Eggy jumped into the yellow Mercedes Boogie had given him, and he took off. He'd been drinking. On Park Heights Avenue near a country club golf course, he lost control of the car. The phone call to Boogie came from his brother Jackie.

"There's been a bad accident," he said.

By the time Boogie got to the scene, an ambulance had taken Eggy away, but the car was still there, thoroughly demolished. Eggy was dead before they got him to a hospital.

"He was my older brother, but he was really my younger brother," Boogie said. "He worked for me, and he looked up to me because I was the bread winner. But there was nothing I could do to get him past the gambling, and the alcohol that went with it. The hardest thing was telling my mother."

Neither he nor Jackie could face up to it. They called Nettie's rabbi, and he broke the news to her.

The death of Eggy gave Boogie one more reason to distance himself from the daily grind of the business. Life ran out for everybody, one way or another. If you did it right, you spent life enjoying yourself, and you spread as much of the joy as you could. The Merry-Go-Round money helped on both counts.

In 1976, two years after Eggy's death, the boxing obsession took Boogie away from the business. Two years later, in the closing weeks of 1978, Boogie stepped away again. Let Harold handle the day-to-day management, he said.

Within a year, this looked like a mistake. The company went with cheaper merchandise, and customers decided they didn't like the fashions. Shopping at Merry-Go-Round wasn't about cost, it was about style, about attitude. In 1979, the company had its least profitable year ever.

Boogie dutifully returned to work and brought in truck loads of designer jeans. Merry-Go-Round immediately quadrupled its bottom line from the previous year. But, a year after that, he was once again restless.

"Lenny was predictable," Mike Sullivan told Baltimore Magazine. "When the company was in trouble, he'd work seventy, eighty hours a week. But, when things were going well, you saw less and less of Lenny." He called the Boogie-Harold relationship "a marriage that came apart."

In the winter of 1981, Boogie told Sullivan he was going to "the islands." On the way, Sullivan recalled, "he stopped off at Turnberry Isle, and he never came back."

An exaggeration, but only a slight one. Boogie discovered Turnberry, the ritzy North Miami hotel and condominium resort, and there he discovered Diane Gabrielle Pepper, thereafter known simply as Pepper.

By this time, Boogie was approaching 40. Pepper was 21. She was born in Germany but in childhood moved to rural Tennessee and grew up there. She learned how to hunt and fish. Her father worked in the restaurant business, so Pepper had jobs serving coffee and tending the salad bar. She was a waitress and a hostess. She did some modeling in her teens. When Boogie spotted her, she was working at the Turnberry Isle Tennis and Racquet Club, located directly below the luxury condo Boogie owned upstairs.

In the '80s, Turnberry Isle was rocking. Fancy restaurants and nightclub. Yachts right outside the apartments, and lots of tennis courts. Jimmy Connors lived in the building. James Caan was there, and Julio Iglesias, and, recalls Pepper, "a lot of Saudis with their suitcases full of money. Piles of hundreds inside suitcases that they'd open up just to pull out the money.

"And that's where I met Boogie," she said one day in the summer of 2021, years after their marriage and three children and divorce. Here her voice broke. She'd lived through the craziness, the quick temper and gambling and the impulsiveness. But she'd held onto affection, and a sense of protectiveness, as well.

"There's only one Lenny Weinglass," she said. "When I talk about him, my heart is so full."

But, love at first sight, this was not.

"When I first knew him, I thought he was the craziest thing I ever saw," Pepper said. "I came from the South, where you had to have manners and respect. Then I'm with somebody who has neither. I was a country bumpkin. He was city. And then, the silly things he'd do…

"One night we went to dinner, and he approached the maitre d' walking on his hands. Or, one night in Miami, we're eating out with another couple. I ordered spaghetti and marinara, and I dripped some sauce on my white blouse. I was embarrassed. He spilled some on his shirt, to make it even. Or we'd sit at a table, and he'd say to people at the next table, 'That looks good,' or he'd go over and take a bite of what they had. They were either shocked or found it hilarious. But he loves the attention, and he loves to make people laugh. I found it all very intoxicating."

Intoxicating, and maddening. He still had the snap temper, which led to occasional fist fights with wise guys. There was a gambling problem that blind-sided her as it worsened. And some fleeting religious issues.

"His brother Jackie didn't like me," Pepper said, "because I wasn't Jewish. Then there was Nettie, who was hilarious. When she met me, she said, 'Leonard, what are you doing? You bring this shiksa here?' He told her, 'No, Mom, her name is Diane Schwartz.' She'd say, 'I know she's a shiksa.'"

Then there was the trip to Tennessee to meet Pepper's parents. He knew Pepper had been born in Germany, though their discussions hadn't gone very deeply into her roots. Driving to her parents' home the first time, Boogie asked, "Is their house heated with gas?"

"Probably," Pepper said. "Why?"

Boogie just looked at her, until it sank in.

"Is this because of my German background?" she asked.

"Sort of," Boogie said. Those long-ago Friday nights, with Nettie lighting the Shabbat candles and weeping over her murdered twin sister, stayed with him.

"Oh, my God, you're killing me," Pepper said.

"How do I know your parents didn't…?"

"Really?" Her parents would have been children during the war.

"I just had to ask," Boogie said.

But the relationship's real trouble was the gambling. He was a child of Solomon Weinglass, who never escaped the card tables. He was the brother of Eggy, who took him into the football betting and then died outrunning the bookmakers. For Boogie, the gambling went back to Benny's Pool Hall, and crazy midnight foot races up Reisterstown Road, and football pools dispensed at City College in the frantic moments before basketball games down in the school gym.

By the time it was over, he estimates more than $60 million in gambling losses.

"Absolutely true," says his attorney, Ray Altman. "A very aggressive gambling addiction."

On any given weekend, somewhere between half a million and one million dollars in bets.

"You can take it all the way back to Benny's," he recalled years later, with millions gone to gambling and two rehabilitation stays behind him. "I'd bet quarters on eight-ball or nineball. Ping pong I'd bet. And Benny would back me. I'm 15 or 16 years old and didn't have any money, but he'd back me. We'd give points sometimes. Benny would say, 'Well, we'll spot you three points.' He knew his ping pong players and his pool shooters."

But, when Merry-Go-Round money came in, the stakes were a lot higher. He told himself he knew what he was doing. He studied box scores and listened to some of the wise guys. Somebody would know about a quarterback's bad knee, or a starting pitcher's aching arm.

"There's a lot of excitement when you're watching Monday Night Football and there's a million dollars riding on it," Boogie reflected. "Believe me, you're paying serious attention to every single play. You win a million, and there's no feeling like it. But you lose a million, and you're up at 3 in the morning, lucky you can cover it but thinking, 'How do I get the million over to the bookmakers,' because they only take it in cash, and they want it in twenties or hundreds, and that's a lot of bills to be carrying out of a bank."

He said this early one evening on his way to a Gamblers Anonymous meeting. The betting was years behind him now, but the gnawing urge still had to be squelched.

"We'd go out to his ranch every year," Ray Altman said. "He'd have this big party for a kids' charity. He was betting real big on baseball back then, but he'd actually bet on anything. He used to walk around with this little clicker. He clicked it, and it gave him the score of every baseball game. And there were lots of them going on at the same time. He felt he was the maven in knowing who was going to win. He lost big-time on that."

"He couldn't enjoy a game," says Allan Charles, "unless he had 50 grand riding on it. So he'd have 50 on a bunch of different games on any given night. One summer, when his kids were little, he took a house in Rehoboth. He had little pagers. That summer, he won $7 million on baseball. The bookies wouldn't take his bets. He'd study box scores, pitchers. He was the Albert Einstein of gambling.

"But it wasn't just baseball. We went to the Super Bowl when the Ravens played the Giants. He had a quarter million bet on the game, and then he bet another quarter on the way down."

Over the years, he'd stayed in touch with Jane Cisar (aka Bunny Nicolle), his first serious girlfriend during the early Merry-Go-Round years in Atlanta. She'd married Bruce Dobbs, a surgeon, and the two of them had grown close with Boogie and Pepper.

In the 1980s, Bruce Dobbs remembers, "Boogie and I would go to Vegas and gamble. Back then, he would gamble, minimum $2,500, up to $25,000. On a hand of blackjack. He had a system, a hybrid. Most people don't know how to bet. 'I feel lucky' is the worst thing. His system, if you won, let the bet ride. Increase each time. When he'd lose, he'd go back to the original bet.

"He'd have his own table in the high roller room. You can walk into the room but not bet unless you bet the big bucks. With his own dealer. I remember leaving all our money on the table and going to dinner, just him and me. We left the table with three chips, $25,000 each. So he's walking into dinner with $75,000 in his pocket like it's nothing."

"I'm going to Vegas one time, about six months after I got married," says Stan (The Fan) Charles, "and I call Boogie because maybe he can get me tickets so Jayne and I can go to Cirque d' Soleil. Boogie says, 'Done,' just like that. So I'm out there, and I get a call, and it's Boogie. 'Where are you now?' 'Vegas.' 'How'd you like to make ten grand?' He says, 'I am so hot right now, I'd like to pay you to bring me some money.'"

He meant his winnings. They amounted, at that moment, to $250,000, which he wished to keep quiet.

Charles went to his new bride and told her about Boogie's call.

"How much does he want you to bring him?" she asked.

"Quarter of a million dollars."

"And how much do you get for this?"

"Ten grand."

"Make it fifteen," said the new bride.

Stan the Fan called Boogie back, and Jayne Charles negotiated the new terms. No problem. Boogie told Stan how to pack the money in a duffel bag. This is under-the-table cash money, and it's before the terrorist attacks, so there's not as much security as later. Put the money under a bunch of towels and underwear, Boogie says. This evening, he explains, you'll meet a fellow. He'll come to your hotel room and he'll give you the money. You get on a small propeller plane and fly the money in Aspen, where Boogie will be waiting.

"A quarter of a million dollars," Charles says, still not quite believing this 20 years later. "The most money I'd ever had was a hundred-dollar bill I got from my uncle, the night before my bar mitzvah.

"So I'm having dinner that evening with Jayne and her cousin, Larry Goldman, and I had to leave early and meet this guy in my hotel room. I'm thinking, What's to keep him from popping me with a gun and taking the money? Here comes a knock, and I open the door, and it's an unassuming guy like Ozzie Nelson, from Ozzie and Harriet. He says, 'Here's the money. Check out how much is here.' You could see it was organized.

"Next morning, I get up early, make my way to the airport, fly on a prop plane where you can't sit with your luggage. There's a dozen people on board and everybody's thrown their luggage up front, where's it's just sitting there. And I'm scared I'll nod off and wake up and, you know, 'Where's my bag?'

"Boogie meets me at the airport in Aspen and takes me to his office. He takes me back to his safe, says, 'Here's the money.' Fifteen grand, sure enough. And he says to me, 'Boy, that Jayne's a tough negotiator.'"

So was Pepper. She and Boogie were living together in Florida, unmarried, when the gambling got too intense for her. They'd been to Aspen a few times for skiing, and loved it, and Pepper said she was moving there.

"We were vacationing in Ocean City, and I told him, 'I can't do this lifestyle any more with you.' He was doing a lot of gambling. I handed him the keys to the Porsche and said, 'I've gotta get out of here.' I still loved him. But the price was too high. So I moved to Aspen."

Hanging with friends back in Baltimore, Boogie told everybody how miserable he felt. He hadn't missed anybody like this since he did his basic training in Kentucky and longed for Joanie. When he decided, eight months later, to propose to Pepper, he flew to Aspen with three engagement rings and told her to pick one.

"He called and said he was coming out," Pepper recalled. "He said losing me was the hardest thing that ever happened to him, and he couldn't get over me. I don't know, maybe getting older, he was ready to settle down. I brought a strong sense of family. I wasn't just a pretty face who got her nails done."

There were several hundred people invited to the wedding, which was held in Aspen. The printed invitation had a line straight out of Baltimorese. It said, "Dress: Matters."

"All the people in Aspen said, 'What does that mean?'" Pepper said. "They didn't get it. Baltimoreans did."

It was straight out of Benny's Pool Hall, or the Hilltop Diner. Short, caustic.

"Your date just walked off with another guy. Gee, too bad."

"Matters."

"A crazy wedding," Pepper recalled. "Giant heads, carnival acts, people from a dance company. It was a show."

Boogie's mom wasn't too crazy about the whole deal. She never got past Boogie bringing home a shiksa. By the time they married, Nettie was suffering early dementia. She sat in the first row as Boogie and Pepper prepared to say their wedding vows. The place was very quiet. Then came Nettie's voice, calling up to her son.

"Label, what are you doing up there?"

He was starting a new life, actually. It was the beginning of Boogie's years in Aspen, and a step further away from the Merry-Go-Round grind. One day he called Mike Sullivan, back in Baltimore.

"How would you like my office?" he said.

"Of course," Sullivan said, "but I don't want to move in and then have you come back."

"I'm not coming back," Boogie said. "And, if I do, I'll take Harold's office."

"Sure," said Sullivan, who'd absorbed a little bit of Baltimore sarcasm by this time.

"Yeah, I mean it, Mike," said Boogie. He hung up and then called back a few minutes later. "Oh, I forgot to tell you the most important thing. You got my title. Now you're president of the company."

Chapter Seventeen

The Donald Meets The Boog

Nestled high in America's glorious Rocky Mountains, Aspen, Colorado, is a shiny little town of about 7,500 citizens where Boogie and Pepper built Merry Go Ranch, a paradise with 10 bedrooms, 9 bathrooms, a full-size indoor basketball court, an indoor track and a tennis court, an indoor racquetball court, swimming pool, game room, steam room, massage room, guest house, eight stables for their horses, and enormous windows through which they could gaze upon 21 manicured acres of nature's unbounded gorgeousness. The home was valued at roughly $50 million.

This is widely considered to be a long way from Violet Avenue in northwest Baltimore.

Towering directly over Aspen is Red Mountain, sometimes known as Billionaire Mountain. Tourists come here for the area's four luxurious ski resorts. Skiing is the very heart and soul of Aspen's sporting life.

It is also a long way from the sporting life at Benny's Pool Hall.

Downtown Aspen consists almost entirely of upscale shopping, high-end restaurants and fancy salons and boutiques, where ordinary folks can spot such celebrities as Michael Jordan, Cher, Jon Bon Jovi, Dan Marino, Goldie Hawn, Charles Barkley, Will Smith, Owen Wilson, and Quincy Jones.

This is a long way from the Hilltop Diner, where the big names included Fat Earl, Fenwick, Eggy and Boogie.

Aspen is a place, GQ Magazine once declared, "that has earned its reputation as the most ostentatious small town in the United States…where people who've never skied before parade around in $2,000 ski suits…where, during the Christmas rush, press agents call ahead to the local papers to drum up more attention for their vacationing clients, supposedly trying to get away from it all."

All of this is a long way from anything seen in scruffy, working class Baltimore—though, not to hear certain Aspen lifers describe it. They have a term for what's happened to their town. Boogiefication, they call it. It is not a term of affection.

It commenced with a place called Boogie's Diner, which Boogie intended to bring a hint of middle class charm amid all the relentlessly high-end Aspen restaurants. And, not to be minimized, to bypass any need for him to wait long minutes in some annoying line.

As Boogie describes it, not long after he and Pepper expressed their wedding vows, they opened a women's clothing boutique. They saw it mainly as a kibitz. One evening, Boogie left the store to grab a quick bite somewhere.

"And everywhere I went," he said, "I had to wait in line like a tourist. So I went out and bought this corner."

He means a one-story building at the corner of Aspen's Cooper and Hunter, just a couple of blocks from the base of ski slopes, for which he paid $1.1 million. He tore down the old wooden structure at that location and put up a 9,000 square foot glass and steel restaurant, which he modestly called Boogie's

Diner. For good measure, he put it directly above a new clothing boutique where people could shop while they waited for a meal. The two operations were connected by stairway and separated only by a glass floor, through which patrons could observe each other celebrating the good life.

Unlike the original single-story structure, the new place was precisely two stories high. Some in Aspen complained about this, quite loudly. They believed it was blocking their full view of the Rocky Mountains.

They complained to local reporters. The mayor took shots at Boogie. Then there was an act of vandalism. Merry-Go-Ranch had a statue of a horse, which some cretin spray-painted. In Aspen, such an act all by itself was considered a crime wave.

The only people who liked Boogie's new venture were all those who packed the place. Boogie's Diner felt like a throwback to another era. It evoked memories of the '50s. On its walls were big photographs of pop icons such as Elvis and Brando and Little Richard. Also, photos of Boogie himself, in his athletic prime. A public address system blared early rock and roll. During lulls, Boogie would grab a microphone and serenade diners with songs from his high school era. No one confused him with Dion.

"It was the only family place in town," said Matti Bourgeault, who became the diner's supervisor (and, later, for a while, Boogie's fiancée). "The average person, it cost $11. Parents wanted to bring their kids, because we had what nobody else had: milk shakes, chicken fingers, apple pie, matzoh ball soup.

"No one else had picked up on the dual experience of dining and shopping. Families would come to town to vacation and go out for dinner, but it's packed. We're doing eleven hundred people a day. So what do they do while they're waiting for a table? They go downstairs and shop.

"The husbands are saying, 'I might as well update my jeans,' and the sales girls are saying, 'Oh, my goodness, your butt looks so cute in those.' We were the largest denim store in the country. We're selling 20,000 jeans a year in only seven months, because those are the only months the tourists come. And every celebrity that came to town showed up: Bill Clinton, Goldie Hawn, Antonio Banderas, Chris Evert."

"Every day, Boogie would go to the diner," said Pepper. "It felt like his old home town, with its pink vinyl booths and French fries swimming in gravy like the old Hilltop Diner. We had nice meals, plus diner food. It was a hangout for local baseball teams and kids and birthday parties."

Goldie Hawn was a regular. Madeline Albright, the former secretary of state, came several times. Later, she recognized Boogie and his third wife, Gail, on the street in Colorado. Imagine a distinguished former secretary of state hailing someone named Boogie.

Directly below the diner, boutique customers could shop for boots from the skin of eight different exotic animals and $3,000 Tibetan lamb coats and Boogies Diner athletic jackets. Sometimes, between the diner and the clothing store, they pulled in six figures in a day. Downstairs alone, they did nearly $8 million a year.

"It was the most popular place in town, on the most dominant corner in town," Boogie said. "And we're in a very busy week one year, around Christmas, and I'm on the floor selling some clothes. I'm wearing a V-neck shirt and jeans. Also, cowboy boots because they gave me some height. And one of my sales people says, 'That guy wants to talk to you.'"

He's pointing toward Donald Trump. This is 1988. Boogie doesn't recognize him at first, but the sales guy whispers, "He said, 'Tell him Donald Trump wants to see him.'"

But Boogie's busy trying to sell a $5,000 leather coat to a customer. He's a little busy. He signals Trump to wait a bit. When they meet, Boogie says, "How can I help you?"

"For Christ's sake, I'm trying to get something to eat," Trump says, smiling. "Can you get us a seat upstairs?"

The place was packed, but Boogie put Trump ahead of some customers who'd been waiting in line. This drew a few boos. As Trump devoured a burger, he took in some of the diner's decorations. These included the 1955 Corvette once owned by Elvis Presley, which Boogie bought and parked inside the diner. When Trump finished eating, and noticed all the action in both places, he approached Boogie once more.

"Got a minute?"

"Half a minute. We're busy."

"I'd like you to open this up in New York," Trump says.

"I can't talk about that now. I'm busy."

Trump's taken aback by this. He's not accustomed to such flippancy, even before his White House days.

"Do you ever come to New York?" Trump asks.

"Every month."

He pulls out a business card and asks, "Would you come up and see me?"

"Sure."

"Call my secretary."

This stops Boogie cold.

"Don, Don," he says, then lapses into his occasional third-person comic reference. "We're getting off on the wrong foot, Don. The Boog does not call secretaries."

He hands Trump's card back to him. Big deal, the phone number was an answering service. So Trump gives him a second card. This one's got a direct line to his office.

A month later, Boogie's in New York on a buying trip. Much too early one morning, his hotel room telephone rings.

"I'm pissed," recalled Boogie, "because my regular people know not to call me too early, and I'm sleeping because I was out the previous night with six of my buyers."

It's Trump on the line. Turns out, he called Boogie's secretary, found out where he was staying, and got the hotel number.

"I thought you were gonna call me," says Trump.

"Who is this?" says Boogie.

"You know who it is."

"Is this Donald?"

"Yeah. Why didn't you tell me you're staying at that hotel? It's one of mine. I'd have put you in a suite."

"I'm still fuckin' sleeping."

"Call me, I'm here," says Trump.

Two days later, Boogie gets around to it. Dressed in torn acid-washed jeans and red cowboy boots, with several days' worth of beard and his hair in a pony tail, he makes his way to Trump Tower. To give himself a slight look of money, he's also wearing a leather jacket worth a few grand.

The jacket does nothing to impress the large security officer standing at the elevator in the lobby of Trump Tower. He looks like a gargantuan killer linebacker.

"Can I help you?" he says, not quite pleasantly.

"I'm here to see Donald Trump."

"What'd you say?"

"I'm here to see Donald Trump."

"Boy, you better get out of here before I put my foot up your ass."

Boogie turns sideways, an old instinct in case he has to run. There's no way this behemoth's going to catch him in a foot race.

"Listen," he says, "before you put that foot up my ass, you better pick up that phone line there. And tell Mr. Trump that Boogie's here to see him."

"What'd you say?"

"You heard me. Tell him Boogie Weinglass is here."

Now, figuring Boogie may be serious, the officer calls upstairs.

"There's a Bogey here to see you."

"It's not Bogey," says Boogie. "It's Boogie."

"Boy, you better not be jiving me."

Then he hears the big guy say, "Yes, boss. Boss, I'm really sorry."

As he escorts Boogie onto the elevator, the officer apologizes and then asks, "What are you, a rock star?"

"Nope. I own a bunch of clothing stores."

For the next hour, though, he owns Donald Trump. The future leader of the free world can't stop trying to impress him. As the elevator doors open to Trump's floor, two stunning young ladies are there to greet him. Each grabs a Weinglass arm. As they guide him to Trump's office, Boogie instinctively tries to get their phone numbers.

He finds Trump sitting behind a large round desk with his back to a wall. He's wearing a dress suit and much gaudy jewelry.

"And I'm thinking," Boogie reflects, "'Here I am in jeans and tee shirt. Am I being disrespectful? Nah, it's just Boog.'"

Trump quickly boasts of some of his real estate holdings. He says Boogie would love New York. Boogie says he's not so sure. Then he tells Trump that they're already partners. Trump looks puzzled. It's a Brooklyn housing development in which Harold Goldsmith, the real estate genius, invested $15 million of his money and $15 million of Boogie's. Together, they own more of it than Trump, who's in for $20 million.

"So now he knows I'm for real," Boogie said, "and he's visibly embarrassed, thinking I was a guy who just owned a diner and one clothing store." By this time, there were many hundreds of Merry-Go-Rounds across the country and several Boogie's Diners, including one at Lexington and 57th in Manhattan. All of this is unknown to Trump.

So he takes Boogie on a little tour. They go to the basement. It's an empty floor set up for retail shops. Boogie thinks, "This is a dog, it's dead real estate."

"I want to give you space down here," Trump says.

"Where are the other tenants?"

"We just started leasing."

Boogie stares at him. Who does this guy think he's dealing with?

"If you showed me space on the main floor, I might have been excited," he says.

"I can give you 5,000 feet, air conditioned," Trump says. "I'll give you a great deal."

Trump can see he's not getting very far. They go back to his floor, to a large conference room with a long table.

"I have some space in Atlantic City," Trump says. "At Trump Plaza. I'd love to show you the space there."

"I have three stores in Atlantic City," says Boogie.

"Really?"

"Ever heard of Steel Pier?"

"Why don't we get in my helicopter?" says Trump. "It's up on the roof. We can get there in half an hour."

"Nah. Not that important for me to see."

The meeting lasted only a few minutes longer, but not before Boogie remarked, "By the way, I've got a Boogie's Diner at 57th and Lexington. And I've got a Merry-Go-Round in the Empire State Building."

With that, he headed for an airport to fly back to Aspen and ponder life without Donald Trump. But he had better things to do there. He and Pepper were now building a family instead of a corporate chain. Merry-Go-Round, under Mike Sullivan's daily guidance, could take care of itself.

The Weinglass family now included Sage, and twins named Bo and Skye. And there were other children who came into his life, and Pepper's, through the Buddy Program, a mentoring operation for needy youngsters across the Roaring Fork Valley. Many of the children came from single-mother homes where money was tight.

Each year, the Buddy Program held a Backyard Bash at Merry-Go-Ranch to raise money. Each year, more money was raised at a 5- mile run, sponsored by Boogie. Each year, much of the Buddy Program money came from the Weinglass family, and from Boogie's Diner's profits.

When they inducted Boogie into Aspen's Hall of Fame, in 2016, Catherine Anne Provine, the Buddy Program's former executive director, said, "He could have just given the money and walked away, but his inner passion for the program came out with all the time he spent. He seemed to want to help every-one who asked him.

"It's surprising," she said, "that we worked together for quite a number of years, and I would hear from the outside, 'Oh, Boogie helped me do this,' or 'Boogie helped my child,' or 'Boogie helped me purchase this equipment that helped me to walk again.' And he never mentioned any of it."

"He's given to so many people, for so many reasons, that he never, ever talked about," added Ted Gardenswartz on the night of Boogie's Hall of Fame induction. "I remember him telling me one time that he wanted to do something good, that he wanted to leave a mark, every day."

At the Hall of Fame banquet honoring him, the big crowd was told, "He's donated millions to his many charities, including institutions like the Buddy Program. But he's also known to have helped many individuals over the years, from disadvantaged youth who needed help with college tuition to medical expenses to those who needed life-changing treatment or surgery they couldn't afford otherwise."

One of them was Dr. Holly Dalhman.

Chapter Eighteen

Spreading the Money Around

When Holly Dahlman was a little girl, she looked in the mirror and saw why strangers on the street stared at her and heartless classmates mocked her. Her face was unlike all others. Boogie Weinglass looked at her and decided in a heartbeat to change her life forever.

She was born with cranial facial deformities and club feet. Across the next two decades, she would endure nearly two dozen operations.

"Visibly abnormal in appearance," she describes her features. She means, when all this was starting. She says this from her office in Baltimore County's Greenspring Station. This is where Dr. Dahlman has her medical practice today, a long way from Aspen, and from humiliation.

She came from working class parents who couldn't afford the profound help their daughter needed. The parents lived apart. Her mother was secretary for a sheriff. Her father went deep into debt paying Holly's medical bills.

"I wanted to be a normal member of society," she said, "but it was pretty difficult." The recitation of those early years is reduced to sentence fragments. "School, yes. Teased a lot. Throughout school. Really big challenge." To explain them in longer phrases is to risk baring old emotions.

Her father lived in Chicago. Her mother moved to Aspen when Holly was in high school. She loved horses, and one summer day in Aspen rode a borrowed horse past a ranch owned by the Dopkin family. The Dopkins were from Baltimore. They knew Boogie and Pepper Weinglass. Carole Dopkin approached Holly and asked if she'd like a summer job working on her ranch.

Holly was there one afternoon when the Dopkins had visitors from Baltimore, Eddie and Pat Cohen. The Cohens were staying in Aspen with Boogie and Pepper. Eddie was an orthopedic surgeon. He looked at Holly, and that evening he spoke to Boogie and Pepper about the girl, and this set off one more conversation.

"My mother got a call from Carole that night," Holly said. "She told my mother, 'I have a friend named Boogie. He wants to know about Holly.'"

A few days later, Boogie dropped by the Dopkin ranch. Holly was there. Her mother got another phone call from Carole Dopkin that night.

"Boogie wants to pay her medical expenses for the rest of her life," said Dopkin.

It felt like a deliverance from the gods.

In 1984, Boogie and Pepper established the Weinglass Foundation, a philanthropic organization that was based at Merry-Go-Round's national headquarters in Baltimore County.

The foundation granted wishes to terminally ill children, assisted people with money problems, gave money to the sick, cut quickly through red tape. As the Baltimore Sun reported, "The foundation doesn't rely heavily on outside donations. Most of the money comes directly from Weinglass and his wife Pepper."

"You know, my mother had nothing," Holly Dahlman said. "She was a single mom. She used to take a day off work every month just to drive me all the way to Denver, a long drive, about four hours each way, just to have the braces in my mouth adjusted because my mouth had to be rearranged by a special orthodontist."

She met Boogie when she was still in high school. The monthly car rides to Denver, 200 miles each way, ended immediately. Boogie paid for airplane tickets every month. Then there were surgery costs. He paid for those. When her high school days were over, Boogie looked at her after she'd had her latest facial operation. It wasn't entirely successful.

"I don't think you're going to the best guy," he said. "I want you to see the best guy in the country. I'll pay for it." There were several more operations over the next few years. Then Holly applied for medical school at Johns Hopkins University.

When she arrived in Baltimore, Ralph Banner greeted her at the airport to chauffeur her wherever she needed to go. Boogie now had a condominium at the Village of Cross Keys, where Holly stayed while she applied for a Hopkins fellowship.

She started medical school at Hopkins the following fall. In Aspen, Boogie and Pepper took her to dinner before she left.

"How are you gonna get around in Baltimore?"

"Take the bus, I guess," Holly said.

"No, you're not gonna do that."

They bought her a car. She'd never had one. When she finished medical school and came home to Aspen, they hung a banner at Boogie's Diner, saying, "Congratulations Dr. Holly Dahlman." It stayed there all summer.

When she started her residency in Baltimore, she was living in a neighborhood considered slightly edgy. Boogie moved her, rent free, into his own place. He and Pepper stayed elsewhere when they were in town.

Living in Baltimore, she sometimes grew homesick. She pondered moving back to Aspen. One day Boogie called. She told him, "I miss my family. I miss the mountains. I'm thinking of moving back."

Boogie talked her out of it. "He told me, 'Aspen doesn't need you. Baltimore needs you more,'" she recalled. "That was what I needed to hear. It was a reminder of my mission to help those who really need me."

Who knows how much he's given away. The man who delivers the Weinglass mail hobbled when he walked. Boogie paid for his hip surgery. He's given huge money to his old elementary school, the Talmudical Academy.

"When we were married," said Pepper, "we'd get thank you notes every day from people he'd helped. I wanted to remodel the kitchen after our kids grew up. He didn't want me to. He said, 'I don't want to spend the money. I'd rather give it away.'"

Rick Balentine, chief of the Aspen Fire Department, recalls a bad fire in 2018 that "left the town very much on edge. They asked me to talk about wildfire danger at the men's club at the Jewish community center. I spoke for an hour, and then Boogie came up to me afterwards and said, 'Is there anything you need right now?'

"I said, 'Yeah, we've got an old, broken-down truck.' He committed right there to fund a new truck. We got one within maybe two weeks. He paid $126,000 to get it. He does a lot of that, and he doesn't tell people. I told him I'd take the fire truck on one condition—that I could put his name on it. Or else I was gonna tell everybody that he did it."

One day came a phone call from someone who'd lost his legs in a car crash. He had a wife and three children. Boogie bought him a van he could control strictly by hand. For extra measure, he sent the entire family to Disneyland for a week. Multiple friends say he's given them down-payment money on new homes. Others talk of new cars he's bought for them. He doesn't ask. He'll tell them, "I just got you a new car."

When Boogie's old high school basketball coach from City College, Jerry Phipps, went to Aspen one year, he unexpectedly bumped into Boogie. Phipps mentioned he was still coaching, and still trying to get kids into college who couldn't afford entrance fees. Boogie immediately wrote him a check.

"In that way," said Phipps, "he's my hero."

He's never forgotten the Associated Jewish Charities in Baltimore for help the organization gave his mother in the family's toughest years. He's given them millions.

"When he was little, he saw how his mother struggled so much, and how much the Jewish community helped out," said Pepper. "That's why he's given back so much."

Joe Blumberg, who used to accompany Boogie on Merry-Go-Round buying trips, talks about going to the Essen Deli in Baltimore for lunch.

"We go to pay the check," said Blumberg. "Boogie sees a bowl sitting on the counter. He says, 'What's that?' Guy says, 'Our main counter man, Kyle, passed out. He's in a coma. He's got four kids.' Boogie gives him a check for $10,000.

"During the holidays, when the Covid virus was so bad and people weren't eating out, he gave everybody who worked at the Essen a thousand bucks. He felt bad they were struggling and it was the holidays. He knows a guy who's got a shoe store and no business during the pandemic. He says, 'Let's go over there and give him some business.' He spent $1,200 on shoes he didn't need, so the guy wouldn't think we're doing charity."

Josh Scheinker, Boogie's financial adviser, says, "We've calculated that, since 2009, he's given away, no joke, over $20 million. He doesn't want to be thanked or recognized. He just cares. It makes him feel good. He believes in karma. If he helps somebody, it adds years to his life.

"Hundreds of people he's supported, hundreds of 'em. Little stuff nobody ever hears about. Friend from high school died, and the guy's daughter reaches out. He paid for the whole funeral. We're wiring money to people non-stop. The girl that cuts his wife's hair"—that's his third wife, Gail—"he built a basketball court in her back yard for her husband. Random acts like that.

"Harold Goldsmith used to say to me, 'He's pissing away all his money. I gotta see that he doesn't lose everything.' Boogie doesn't see it as pissing it away. The list doesn't end. How about the woman he bought a new wheelchair-accessible van? How about…?"

How about Amanda Boxtel?

Boogie read about her in a newspaper. She was 24 years old, from Brisbane, Australia, skiing in Aspen when she crashed into a tree in February, 1992. The collision shattered four vertebrae. She lost all movement and sensation below her pelvis.

Two weeks after the accident, a doctor walked into her hospital room and said, "You'll never walk again."

The doctor was wrong. Boxtel not only walks, she's become a missionary of hope for all those facing paralysis.

She does it with the aid of a device worn around the waist and legs to allow people with spinal cord injuries to stand and walk using a motorized function.

It's the Weinglass money that got this started and kept it going. A year after her accident, she wanted to get back on her feet again. Maybe leg braces would work. But they would cost $13,000, far beyond her means. She sent out letters to several people in Aspen known to be generous. Only one responded.

"Hi, Amanda," said a voice on her telephone. "This is Boogie. I want to give you the full amount."

"I still have a photograph from that time," she said. "He and Pepper both came down to the hospital and saw me stand tall in my leg braces. The fact that they came down just captured my heart.

"From that time on, he's been an angel in my life. I had this big wheelchair and it was too large for me and I needed something manageable and my insurance didn't consider it a necessity. So Boogie brought me to his house, and there was Pepper, and there were the kids, and there was this new wheelchair."

He bought her a van she could maneuver strictly by hand. He bought her a condominium, where she's lived for the past two decades. He charges her a nominal monthly rent, which goes back to the Weinglass Foundation for further passing along.

"I was living in a one-bedroom apartment, and Boogie came to visit," she recalled. "He said, 'We need to get you something more accessible.' He went looking for places. He really thought about it. He said, 'I want you to have a garage so you can park your car and not have to scrape off any snow. I want you to have easy access to get around.' He really thought about it.

"I'm in awe of my darling Boogie, and I'm amazed by him," she says three decades after first meeting him. "So much of my life comes back to the beauty of Boogie and his heart. He's my angel. And he's taught me the importance of giving back."

She's clearly done that.

She's the founder and executive director of the Bridging Bionics Foundation, which raises money for research and development of bionic technology. Boogie's donated six figures every year. She co-founded a skiing program called Challenge Aspen that grew into a multi-million dollar non-profit. In 2018, she was named a "CNN hero." She teaches skiing. She's delivered speeches that have raised millions of dollars and inspired those neurologically challenged to walk with robotic assistance, the way Amanda walks.

And one other thing: She also skis again.

Chapter Nineteen

Change of Life

Can life get any better than this?

Boogie and Pepper are raising their three kids on God's 21 acres of Eden itself, to which they've added horses and ducks and goats to the existing elk and bears and foxes. The whole family falls in love with Aspen, and much of the town falls in love with them, except maybe those die-hards still claiming Boogie's Diner blocks their view of the Rocky Mountains.

He's charitable beyond the counting. He sponsors Aspen's annual five-mile race benefitting the Buddy Program and hosts Boogie's Bash at his ranch. These events alone help raise millions for needy kids. He spreads around some serious college tuition money. And he's still bankrolling untold pals from the old days back in Baltimore.

He spends many of his days hanging out at Boogie's Diner, where he turns shmoozing into an art form. As he moves among the tourists eating their burgers and fries, he points out the celebrity pictures hanging on the walls.

"Never mind Elvis, you see that handsome kid over there? That's me," he says. "Did you see the Barry Levinson movie,

'Diner?' I'm the real Boogie. I'm the guy Mickey Rourke played."

Then, if they seem interested, he gives listeners some personal background, skipping lightly around the football pools and the blank report cards and the swiped police cars, focusing mainly on his basketball exploits back in Baltimore.

The game's still in his blood. He coaches a girls' basketball team for a while. For ten years he coaches the boys junior varsity basketball team (and assists the varsity coach) at Aspen High School. He travels on the team bus. He does overnight trips to distant schools. He's got to be the only high school jayvee coach in America who's worth a few hundred million dollars.

"They never had a good team before I got there," he says. "Team full of skiers, and no black guys. They'd play teams outside of Aspen and never even had a .500 record. My first year coaching the jayvee, we went undefeated."

Can life get any better than that?

In Aspen, the living's so good that it draws an unanticipated newcomer: Harold Goldsmith. In 1981, he moves his new wife, the former Beth Himmelstein, and their son, Josh, to Aspen. His life's gotten over-programmed back in Baltimore, and he needs to downshift a little.

Like Boogie, he's put the daily Merry-Go-Round business into the background. Mike Sullivan's running the show now, with Boogie and Harold mostly cheering from the sidelines. But, unlike Boogie, happily coaching basketball and kibitzing at the diner, Harold continues his manic money-making.

He takes over Eastern Savings Bank, a Baltimore thrift which he converts into a $400 million operation. He becomes the youngest chair in the history of Baltimore's Associated Jewish Charities campaign and raises $12 million there. He goes through a couple of near-misses: publishes a men's magazine,

Fast Lane, which never gets out of the starting blocks; tries to buy Baltimore's News American newspaper, which folds before he can get his hands on it.

He's making lots of money but burning himself out. Maybe Aspen can give him a sense of perspective. He joins an exclusive club there. He gets fixated on his health. He takes up skiing and hiking and biking. And he and Boogie continue to do their little tango. They're contentious brothers who tick each other off but understand how much they've enriched each other's lives.

Meanwhile, over the next decade, Merry-Go-Round's thriving. Sullivan's sticking to his original plan for expanding to 1,500 stores. He's getting closer. He's absorbed DJ's for young men, Cignal for baby boomers, Attivo for men, and then half a dozen more names.

Then, when Merry-Go-Round stock drops a few dollars a share, Sullivan blames it on rumors that he's looking to take on yet another existing chain—"the sort of gossip," as Baltimore Magazine puts it, "that always depresses stock price for a while." It'll pass, Sullivan assures everyone.

Meanwhile, Boogie's Diner is such a hit, they open several replicas, starting with Chicago and Washington, D.C.

Can life get any better than this?

No.

It can only get worse.

Boogie's gambling is now off the charts, and it's killing his marriage. Old friends Jane and Bruce Dobbs fly from their home in San Francisco to try to counsel him. They take Pepper's view: the gambling is ruining everything.

"He'd gamble on anything," says Dr. Bruce Dobbs. "I mean, he didn't care what it was. 'Sweden's playing Ireland in field hockey? Great, let's get a bet down.'"

When he and Pepper go to Las Vegas, which is too often for her taste, Boogie takes over an entire table in the high-stakes room. He bets ten grand at each chair, on each hand. He loves it when crowds gather to watch him.

Any time they go to a restaurant, anywhere at all, and there's no television available, they get out of the place fast. He needs ESPN so he can see who's winning and who's not. When they spend some time each summer in Ocean City, Md., Pepper awakens each morning to find Boogie with a legal pad and a newspaper in front of him. Every line of the legal pad is filled with that day's bets. The money's bigger each day than most people make in a year.

"It's an addiction," she tells him.

"I got it figured out, Pep," he says. "If you do this, and you double down…"

"You can talk until you're blue in the face," she says, "but…"

"No, no, I got it under control."

Voices rising, emotions overlapping, and every syllable tearing up the remains of a marriage.

Old friend Stewart Levitas remembers vacations in Dewey Beach, where Boogie had money on all 16 major league baseball games every day, $25,000 on each game.

"The men on base kind of thing," Levitas said. "While the games were going on, it'd report the scores, the men base, everything, and he'd click the pager and go game to game. He had this thing in his hand, hour after hour.

"We went to that first Ravens Super Bowl, against the Giants. He bet $250,000 on the Ravens, and then another $60,000 at halftime. So he won $310,000. The morning after the game, I find him sitting at a dining room table with a yellow legal pad and the names of all his employees at Boogie's Diner, and how much he's going to give each one of them, thousands of dollars each. Who does that? But that was the first thing on his mind."

The money itself became a blur. In the aftermath of therapy—two extended trips to rehab, actually - Boogie estimates he gambled away somewhere north of $60 million. There's a kind of perverse pride in the number. Yes, it's a lot. But, implicitly, the message is: "Look how I could afford it!"

Levitas remembers a country club card tournament, where he told Boogie about whispers that he'd lost $1 million gambling. Boogie's response? "Stew, why didn't you say something? I told you, it was $2 million.'"

Matti Bourgeault, who became president of Boogie's Diner's retail side, said, "He'd be coaching basketball, and we'd go on the road. He had to have the newspapers right away. He was always checking his bets. We had to get him help."

"He'd tell me he was really good at it," says Pepper. "And I'd say, 'Yeah, you are. But you're still losing a fortune.'"

Losing a marriage, as well. "The gambling," says Pepper, "was the demise of our marriage. It took him away from me and the kids. We had to get him help, but it was already too late for the marriage."

Every Vegas casino had his name on a list: The Sands, The Mirage, MGM, all of them. He'd go to one casino after another. Part of it was superstition, and part was theory: if you're losing, go somewhere else. But where do you go when you've used up every place in town?

You go for help.

Pepper gathered a bunch of friends, and one evening Boogie walked into an intervention. The marriage was all but done, but maybe she could save Boogie from himself. Eight or ten people in the room, including a professional. They told him he was out of control. They told him they cared about him.

They said he was jeopardizing his wife and kids, his home, his business. He assured them he wasn't. They told him he was tearing down everything he'd worked his whole life to build. He listened to none of it.

Then they laid down the law. If he didn't go to rehab, they'd go to some judge and freeze all his assets so he had no access to his money. Simple as that.

So he goes to rehab, though he's not really buying into it. Goes to a place called Sierra Tuscon, out in the Arizona desert, where the heat's routinely around 115 degrees. It's rehab for rich people with addictions: gambling, drugs, alcohol, sex. Thousand dollars a day, and no insurance coverage, and you stick around for 30 days.

Boogie figures, thousand bucks a day, big deal. He bets ten times that much on a single hand of blackjack. This will be a smile, even when it's not.

"It was very humbling at first," he remembers. "Very, very humbling. First you go in, and they strip you of all your clothes. To make sure people with drug addictions aren't hiding anything in their socks or something. And it's in your room, lights out, by 9:30, and then you're up at 6:30 in the morning. Not my lifestyle at all."

But he does his best, in his lunatic fashion. He does an hour-long intake interview with a medical doctor who's in her thirties, "beautiful as a movie star," and naturally, this being Boogie, he decides to hit on her. This does not work out.

"But I took my shot," he says later.

Early in the stay, he's got a real itch to get a bet down on a pro football game with an eight-point spread. He'll take the points, always loves taking the points. All phones are strictly off limits, though. So he breaks into an administrator's office, grabs the phone, and crawls under a desk so he can place a bet without some rat turning him in.

Then there are classes. A yoga class, with a pretty instructor. Naturally, he hits on the yoga instructor. He climbs over a ten-foot fence to take an unscheduled dip in the swimming pool. What the hell, it's hot out there. He goes to all the classes, and hangs in for 30 days, but when he leaves there's still a sense that this rehab hasn't fully kicked in. Pepper understands this. Not long after he gets home, the marriage has essentially run its course.

"Twenty years together, married 16 years," Pepper reflects on a summer afternoon years later. "I still get choked up, I still care so much. He's a crazy, loving, giving man. There's never gonna be anybody like him. But it was all too much for the marriage."

Does it get any worse than this?

Yes.

Much worse.

On February 13, 1991, Harold's in Las Vegas, where he's trying to take over a casino there. He's nurtured such a dream for a long time. He had it when he was still married to Rona Smith, his first wife, back when they made their living on the Goldsmith rental properties.

"Even in the early days," says Rona, "he'd talk about casinos. If Merry-Go-Round hadn't come along, Harold never would have gone into such a business. Merry-Go-Round was really Boogie. In a million years, Harold wouldn't have gone into the clothing business."

"Harold called it the rag business," says Ray Altman, who was one of Merry-Go-Round's attorneys. He was friends with both men since their Hilltop Diner nights. "He wasn't proud of just spending his life selling clothes to kids. He wanted something more intellectual."

Altman and Weinglass share a recollection—of Boogie imploring Harold to stay away from any hostile take-over attempts in Las Vegas.

"I don't think Harold knew who he was dealing with," Altman says. "I know they were not happy when he took over. He controlled the board, and he was going to change what they were doing. They were guys who'd had this business for years, and they didn't like this little Harold Goldsmith from Baltimore taking over. And he was not shy. When he thought he had control, and did have it, he executed it. He was going to do what the hell he wanted to do.

"And I remember Boogie telling him, 'Harold, don't do it. You don't know who you're dealing with. You're gonna be real sorry you ever started up with these people.' And Harold didn't accept that. 'Nah, I'm smarter than any of those guys,' that was his attitude."

"I fought him for days over this," Boogie recalls. "We were partners in everything, but I said I don't want any part of this. I figured it was terrible karma for me, with my gambling issues. And I figured these are not the kind of people you want to get hostile with."

Harold wasn't listening. He was in Vegas, on the phone with Mike Sullivan. Merry-Go-Round was planning a stock offering, and they needed to pick an underwriter. Boogie was in Florida. Sullivan suggested a conference call. Harold said no, it was late, and he wanted to get back to Aspen while it was still daylight. So he got off the phone and ran for the airport.

The flight to Aspen was brief, but the landing took away three lives. Harold was the only passenger. The small, chartered Lear jet approached Aspen's airport, Sandy Field, in the midst of a sprinkly early evening snowfall and a cover of only 1,000 feet. Federal rules instruct pilots not to land at Aspen using instruments when the ceiling is less than 3,100 feet above the runway. The Aspen tower manager, Joseph Saladino, told the Baltimore Sun it was up to the pilot at that point.

"We can only advise him of weather conditions," he said.

The plane's captain, Harold E. Ravnsborg, was headed southeast over the airport when he spotted the control tower. He banked sharply right, flew northwest parallel to the airport, then banked right again, trying to make a U-turn.

An air traffic controller later said the pilot came in too low and banked too sharply. He was still two miles from the airport tower when the plane began shuddering and its nose pitched forward. The plane's wings began to tip back and forth. At 5:41 p.m. with one wing pointing almost straight down, the wing hit the ground all by itself.

The plane bounced and then burst into a ball of flames as it skidded several hundred yards and finally stopped—about one mile below Boogie's ranch.

Boogie was in Miami, with Pepper and the kids, when he heard the news. One of Merry-Go-Round's accountants called him.

"They fucking killed him," Boogie said. The words just leaped from him. He knew about tough guys and money. He knew about gamblers he'd crossed through the years, and the threats they'd issued against him, and against Eggy who lost all control of the car that final night. And now Harold. More tough guys and money, he thought. Vegas tough guys, and this time the money was bigger than ever. That's where his mind went: it couldn't have been an accident.

His mind went back to arguments they'd had over preceding weeks.

"They're not gonna let a little Jewish guy from Aspen take over this casino," he said. "This is not Pikesville."

"Boog, you think everything's cowboys and Indians," Harold said. "It's not. These guys are on the New York stock exchange."

"So what? The biggest crooks in the world are on the New York stock exchange."

Rona Smith was in Baltimore when she heard the news. She heard it from her son Adam, the son she'd had with Harold, who called from Colorado. He was a student at the University of Denver. He heard about the crash on the radio. When she hung up the phone with Adam, Rona had to call Julie, the other child she had with Harold, who was a student at Syracuse University.

Who knows what caused the crash? Boogie has his instincts, and others have their own. There are friends who blame pilot error, though the pilot was a veteran who'd flown Goldsmith previously. Some blame icing. Some say the plane simply banked too sharply and stalled out.

Mark Huffman, who covered the crash for the Aspen Times, later reported there was no black box on the plane, only a tower recording of the pilot's last words: "Fucking stall."

More than a thousand people crowded into Baltimore's Chizuk Amuno synagogue for Harold's funeral service. Boogie was one of the pallbearers. Then, for several days, he sat shiva for his old partner.

And then, four years later, he began sitting shiva for Merry-Go-Round.

Chapter Twenty

When the Merry-Go-Round Stopped

When Merry-Go-Round shuts down, Boogie and Harold are long gone from the beating heart of it. Over the previous dozen years, Boogie retired, briefly un-retired, and retired again a couple of times. And Harold's been gone since his plane crash four years earlier.

They'd written retail history when they were both running the show. They were the industry's Lennon and McCartney, they were Butch and Sundance. But then they were gone. With one gone, Merry-Go-Round was just another clothing outlet. With both gone, it was just a matter of time before closure.

They'd long since turned over control of the company to Mike Sullivan, but even Sullivan was gone by now. He arrived in 1974 and assumed increasing influence when Boogie first retired in 1982. Then Sullivan took on more power when Harold died in February, 1991.

Eight months after Harold's death, the corporation's stock price fell 13 percent, and a year later sales fell 18 percent. But Sullivan, sticking to his original game plan of 1,500 stores, grabbed 450 Chess King outlets—for a reported $46.2 million - in May, 1993.

This was the beginning of the end. Eight months later, January of '94, Merry-Go- Round filed for Chapter 11 bankruptcy protection. Reaching for some of the old magic, the company brought Boogie out of retirement. This was part sentiment, part desperation. But it was already too late—for the company, and for any Weinglass magic. Customers had lost interest, and the banks had lost faith.

Within days, Fidelity Investments of Boston bought $90 million of Merry-Go-Round debt for 85 cents on the dollar. Within months, the company reported a $62 million loss for the first half of the year and announced plans to close a few hundred of its stores.

Weeks later, Boogie announced he was retiring again—and Sullivan was let go as president. New officers were brought in, and failed to stop the bleeding. That was November of '94. A month later, the company closed more stores and laid off 800 workers.

As the Baltimore Sun described it, "After a two-year struggle to emerge from bankruptcy protection, the chain of apparel stores lost about $200 million and had nowhere to turn anymore. The retailer was spurned by lenders, vendors and, ultimately, shoppers...Even at a time when many retailers are going bankrupt, few have seen any like Merry-Go-Round's."

Boogie was home in Aspen when the end came. "It's like losing a member of the family," he said. "It's depressing. Nothing, I guess, lasts forever."

At the company's Joppa headquarters, much of the immediate blame fell upon the shoulders of the latest CEO, Richard Crystal. A few years earlier, he'd been hired as the firm's fourth chief executive in two years. On the morning the firm's death was announced, Crystal had to be protected by armed security guards.

But there was plenty of blame to spread around, including a lengthy piece ten months later in Fortune Magazine headlined, "The Man Who Boogied Away A Billion."

It was a snarky headline built around a nickname, but it incorrectly implied the blame all fell on one man's shoulders.

"Human history has produced exactly one Johann Sebastian Bach, one Sir Isaac Newton, and—for better or worse—one Leonard 'Boogie' Weinglass," Fortune reporters Justin Martin and Therese Eiben wrote.

"Weinglass is a true original—a streetwise Baltimore bad boy who grew up to be, by turns, hippie, founder of a successful retail chain, multimillionaire, jet-setting Florida playboy, unorthodox Aspen family man, and spectacular failure.

"What a ride...a $1 billion nationwide chain with nearly 1,500 stores and 15,000 employees, Merry-Go-Round became a Wall Street darling, and big-time players like Fidelity Investments, Bear Stearns, and Donald Trump tried to horn in on the action...All that remains is the question...How could something so strong go so wrong?"

The magazine offered a few general answers, none laying the blame on one man: "growing distance from customers, a disastrous acquisition, an insular corporate culture, a string of top management shakeups."

Years after the fall, the memory still stung.

"Very painful," Boogie said one summer afternoon in 2021. "Thousands of people lost their jobs. And these were dedicated, loyal people. We weren't just a corporate thing. I hung out with these guys, I hired them when they were right off the street and promoted a lot of them to buyers and supervisors. They grew up with me. And then, what the stockholders lost..."

At the end, the Merry-Go-Round stock was worthless. Those stockholders who'd made money through the years suddenly found their investments gone. That included Boogie, who lost an estimated $40 million.

He blamed himself for some of this. He'd stopped paying serious attention. When the company was riding high, and he'd already slipped into retirement, he'd still show up a few times a year for the major shows where he'd pick out the jeans and sweaters and other big buys to pitch for the next six months.

After a while, though, he'd leave it to others to make the fashion selections. And fashions were always changing.

As Fortune Magazine put it: "Merry-Go-Round's merchandising style had always been to pick a hot fashion item and then run like mad with it. That had worked fine when the company was smaller, and the clothing market sound. But by 1992, Merry-Go-Round was a national chain of more than 800 stores facing the inherent challenge of meeting the needs of a geographically diverse customer base."

And then the 800 figure went to 1,500—and Merry-Go-Round's core customers went elsewhere.

"From the hip-hop and ethnic looks we carried," Boogie said, "we turned a lot of middle America off. They weren't comfortable walking into a store playing rap music."

In 1993, Melville Corp. offered up its 450-store Chess King chain. They'd offered it twice before, but Merry-Go-Round wasn't buying. Harold was still alive for the first offers, and he thought it was a terrible idea. The chain's merchandise was inferior and its sales were flat. Boogie agreed with him: Stay away.

Harold was gone by '93, but Boogie was still arguing against the deal. Chess King was pitching to the same youth market as

Merry-Go-Round—and, in a lot of cases, doing it in the same malls.

But, as Fortune's writers, put it, "With one eye on Wall Street, the other on a moribund fashion market, the chance to grow by 45 percent overnight held the allure of a siren song."

What the magazine did not report was any behind-the-scenes agonizing between Boogie and Merry-Go-Round's newest ruling class.

"They kept saying to me, and this is exact conversation, 'Boog, you've already made your money. Let us buy Chess King and turn it around.'"

As a sitting member of the board of directors, he still had some say. Finally, though, he couldn't say no.

"A major, major, major, major mistake," he told Fortune's writers. "I could kick myself in the butt."

As Chess King's troubles began to drag down Merry-Go-Round, and sales slowed, and stock values plummeted and bankruptcy ensued, the company was bleeding even more money into attorneys, financial advisers, banks, clothing vendors, bankruptcy professionals.

"It was never the same after Harold died," Boogie recalled. "I got depressed, for sure. And I backed away even more than I had. He was the sledge hammer, he's the one that would have stood by me, saying, 'No, don't take on Chess King.'"

"His attention was elsewhere," his financial adviser Josh Scheinker said. "He built his empire and then gave up too much control, and the people who took his place weren't him. He took his foot off the gas to enjoy his life."

The demise of Merry-Go-Round signaled the end of an era—and one more sign of Boogie's life coming apart: the end of his marriage, the death of his old partner, and the deepening gambling addiction.

Into these shadows, one day he found a new love: Matti Bourgault, a newcomer to Aspen. In her youth, in Maine, she'd been a champion gymnast. She moved to New York, but bailed out after the 2001 terrorist attacks and moved west. Boogie found her at a local athletic club, where they were both working out. She was stretching. He was ogling. They went to dinner that evening, and spent the next six years together.

"He was cute," she says, "but I fell in love with his energy, and he's funny and fun, and he's street smart, and he's got the biggest heart in the world. He was always taking care of people. We had people at the store self-conscious about their teeth, or their ears sticking out, or whatever. He was always helping them. Or buying a piano for some kid who had talent but no money. I couldn't believe how there were always a ton of thank you notes coming to the house."

Three years into it, they were engaged to be married.

She also became attached to Boogie and Pepper's children.

"It was tough for them to have a new person come into their lives," Matti said. "But they were great. For Boogie, it was important that they know about his background. I mean, all that wealth didn't just happen. They were young teenagers by this time. He wanted them to know where he came from. He took them to Baltimore and drove them to his old neighborhoods to make sure they knew how much it took along the way."

Merry-Go-Round was gone, but the Boogie's Diners and the connected boutiques were still thriving. Eventually, Matti became president.

"Boogie was still the best in the business at retail," she said. "He's amazing in fashion. You'd never look at the guy and say, 'He's the fashionista.' But he can walk into a place and pick 'em out. We'd go into showrooms and they'd go through the motions of showing us stuff, and he'd say, 'What about this?' And they'd say, 'Yes, that's our best-selling item.' It's just innate, it's instinct. A kid from Baltimore who came from nothing, but he knows what the whole country wants to wear."

As ever, though, the biggest thing Boogie couldn't control was himself.

"I'd heard rumors that he liked to bet," Matti said, "but I didn't know the extent of it. We'd be at the store, and he'd make phone calls. He said he was checking figures. But he was checking on his bets. His life was consumed by it. We had to get him help."

He went back to Sierra Tuscon. Matti took him there, and then brought him home. He left ahead of schedule.

"He got booted out," she says. "Well, he broke out at first. He and some divorce attorney from Houston, they jumped the fence instead of going to a therapy session. They broke out, and they got reprimanded for it. They said, 'What do we do with this problem child?'

"I was staying at a hotel near the rehab place. They saw this wasn't working for him, so they suggested I do the therapy, so at least I'd know what I was dealing with when we got home."

Wonderful! So now Matti's going to therapy sessions every day, and Boogie's dropped out and taken her place at the hotel where she'd been staying. She's taking classes, and he's sitting by the hotel pool all day.

"It was like, 'What's wrong with this picture?'" Matti said.

But she remembers the moment that finally got to Boogie. They were in Las Vegas on a business trip. He was walking through some hotel casino, and Matti was upstairs in their room when he walked in, "totally distraught."

"You okay?" she asked.

"No," he admitted.

"What happened?"

"I was on the phone with Sage," his daughter, then about 20 years old. "I put her on hold to make a bet."

"Oh, Boogie…"

"And I never got back to her."

That's when he knew he was out of control: the gambling had finally touched him beyond memories of his father sitting in those smoke-filled rooms in West Baltimore, unable to give up the card games while his mother struggled to keep a few dollars ahead of the bill collectors; touched him even beyond Eggy, pursued by angry bookmakers until he crashed his car rounding that curve in Northwest Baltimore.

This time, he'd left his child waiting for him to come back.

It wasn't long after that, Boogie says, that he made the phone calls that finally ended the gambling.

"I'll tell you when I knew I was done gambling," he said, years later. "I called my old bookies."

They were all over the place, in Vegas, in Baltimore, in different locations inside the same cities.

"If you ever take a bet from me again, and I lose, I'm not paying you," he said.

"Then I won't take your bet," the bookies told him.

"That's the point," he said.

"Then the hell with you," they said.

And it was over.

"I lost a lot of money over the years," he would reflect many times. "Lots of money. Millions and millions. I was lucky I could afford to lose. But most people can't. They lose their homes, their cars, they lose their families. Or guys get their arms and legs broken. They tell their friends, 'I need a few bucks, I swear I'll pay you back.' But they can't pay 'em, and no one will lend you, including the banks. I've seen it. Or some of 'em, they wind up jumping off a tall building."

For half a century, Boogie's financial advisors have been Jerry and Josh Scheinker, father and son, from Legg Mason. The father started 55 years ago, and the son stepped in 23 years ago.

"He still feels the need for action every day," says Josh Scheinker, "but now it's all directed at the stock market. It keeps his mind fresh. He stays up with the research and loves it. And he happens to be super sharp at it. I've been on the phone with him where he's made a trade and gained $1 million in an hour, just making a huge bet. He's whip smart.

"But his biggest pleasure is helping people. I've sent out the money. There are hundreds of people he's supported. We're wiring money to old friends non-stop. He just paid off an old friend's mortgage. You and I will never know anybody like him the rest of our lives.

"And you know the biggest bet he's ever made? He's challenged life. Anything thrown at him, he's faced up to it."

In the new century, there was plenty of that.

Chapter Twenty One

High Over America

The new century brought love and dying in equal measure. There was new love with a woman named Sandy St. John. But then, like hammer blows in the night, came Boogie's struggle to stay alive—and Sandy's surrender.

They met through Boogie's children. The kids were Sandy's students when she taught kindergarten at Aspen Country Day School. They adored her. Sandy was married then, and Boogie was married to Pepper. It was only later, in the wreckage of other relationships, that their friendship turned into romance.

"Very sweet, kind person," Pepper remembered years later. "And very kind to my children, who loved her. And I know Lenny cared for her a lot. He stood by her."

At first glance, they made the oddest coupling since the mating of Boogie and Harold Goldsmith. Sandy was an honors graduate of William & Mary College, and Boogie was the former street kid who scrapped his way through high school. She was shy. He loved the entire world's attention. For years, they never took their feelings past friendship.

"A wonderful, beautiful lady," Boogie reflected in the summer of 2021. "When she walked into a room, other than her looks, you wouldn't know she was there, she was so unassuming."

His marriage to Pepper ended in 1999, and his relationship with Matti Bourgault came next. When that engagement ended, Boogie rediscovered Sandy.

"A diamond in the rough," he said. "She educated me. You know, I was never an English major. I wrote her a note one time, and I used 'to' instead of 'too.' Like, 'I love you, too.' She did this kind of stuff, and did it in a nice way, 'cause she was an educator, and Boog was Boog."

He remembers a long afternoon hike, just the two of them, which started out as a friendship and ended as something else.

"It lasted about five hours," he said. "And we talked a lot, and laughed, and by the time it was over, I was in love with her. And the love lasted a long time."

The first years were lovely, and included much talk of marriage. But the last years were torture.

First his, then hers.

An old friend, Dr. Sylvan Feldman, found some troubling lumps during a dental checkup and sent Boogie to Johns Hopkins Hospital. The news was awful: cancer in the throat and tongue. Feldman's early catch might have saved Boogie's life.

He went through three stays at New York's Sloan Kettering Cancer Institute. Once, he spent two months there, heavily drugged, living on I.V. fluids, in acute pain any time he had to swallow. The romance with Sandy was becoming an afterthought for each of them. His kids came to see him, and so did ex-wives and old friends. Each time seemed like the final time.

"It was absolutely horrible for him," said Jane Dobbs. When she looked at him, she could barely remember the early days in

Atlanta, and the first little Merry-Go-Round there, when they were both very young and danced together through endless evenings.

"It was awful just to look at him with the cancer," she said. "He was in such pain, and nothing took it away."

"It was terrible," said her husband, Dr. Bruce Dobbs. "Imagine the worst sore throat you've ever had, and quadruple it 24 hours a day. It was so sad to see, so painful."

His weight, normally approaching 160 pounds, dropped to 126. He looked like an ancient, cadaverous man. Those who saw him anticipated the end—and so did Boogie.

"I thought, 'This is it,'" he said. "I was in so much pain, and they had me on the 18th floor of the hospital. The only reason I didn't jump out the window was that it wouldn't open. So I tried to break it open with a chair. Believe me, I went to the window more than once. You're on those drugs, you're not thinking logically. But I definitely thought the end was near."

As he eventually started incremental improvement, more people came to see him. The hospital allowed two visitors at a time. Sometimes, he'd have a dozen.

"The nurses went ballistic," he laughed later. "Go figure, Boogie breaking the rules."

He's laughing about it in retrospect. It sustains the rebel image. But, when they released him from the hospital, he was still in raw, unrelieved pain and struggling for any signs of improvement.

For a few months, he came back to Baltimore and stayed with attorney Ray Altman and Ray's family. They helped him through some of the worst of it.

He spent several weeks at Jane and Bruce Dobbs' home in San Francisco. Then he spent several more weeks in Santa

Barbara, at Matti Bourgeault's new home. Their romance was over, but deep affection remained.

"He was busy dying, just withering away," Matti remembered. "We got him over to UCLA Hospital so they could look at him there. By this time, he was starting to eat solid food, so I figured, 'Let's get him anything he wants, McDonald's, Kentucky fried chicken, anything.' I figured, 'I don't know if this is good for him, but we gotta get something in him.' He was gaunt. He wanted to gain weight, but it wasn't happening.

"He started walking when he was with me, and he started going to a gym. He wanted to live. He stayed with me for about six weeks. He started getting a little better. But, when I put him in a cab to go back home, I thought, 'Am I ever gonna see him again?'"

The sickness—and time itself - had taken their toll on the romance with Sandy. They loved each other, but it was closer to friendship than passion as the end neared.

"They were great years with Sandy," Boogie said, "until they weren't. She had classy friends. We went to the movies, to the theater, we went hiking, we made love. Over the years, she never moved in totally. I said, 'Keep your place, it's five minutes away, and we'll spend a few nights at each house. And we made love one night, and the next morning she's making breakfast for us, and we're making small talk.

"And this sweet woman says something completely out of context with her personality. She says, 'I don't give a fuck what you think.' She'd never, ever talked like that. And she was really nasty. So I went back to my house, really upset, 'cause I loved her, and I didn't know what the hell's going on.

"Two hours later, my phone rings. It's Sandy. She's at the hospital. She went driving, and she swiped three different cars, and her head's all banged up."

He found her in the hospital's emergency room. The doctors did a biopsy and found a malignant brain tumor.

"That was the cause of her talking to me like that. It was her brain tumor, it wasn't her. I knew something was wrong."

He chartered a plane to take her from Aspen to a more sophisticated hospital in Denver. But the tumor was too advanced for Denver. So they transferred her to the cancer center at Duke University. She was there for a few months, and Boogie stayed with her.

He was still dealing with his own lengthy recovery. He moved Sandy to Naples, Fla., and bought her an apartment. Later, as the end neared, he set up a home hospice for her. He took care of her financial needs to the end.

Meanwhile, waging his own struggle to regain his health, he came back to Baltimore and started seeing a few old friends. One of the old friends was Chip Silverman. They went back to days at Forest Park High School and nights at the Hilltop Diner.

Chip was a keeper of the old stories. He'd played a small role in "Diner" and wrote a book about that era. He'd had his own storied career. He coached the lacrosse teams at Morgan State University and the University of Baltimore. He became the first white assistant dean at the majority-black Morgan State. He helped run Maryland's Drug Abuse Administration.

Now retired, Chip was now living at Boogie's old condominium at Baltimore's Cross Keys development. With him was a striking blonde who'd grown up as Gail Groves in Orlando, Fla.

She'd studied classical ballet for 20 years and then taught dance. She arrived in Baltimore with a husband who'd gotten a full scholarship at the Johns Hopkins University, to go for his doctorate in astrophysics. They later divorced.

In Baltimore, she worked in health clubs and taught aerobics while continuing her education. Then she managed cardiac rehabilitation and wellness programs for the Lifebridge Health and Fitness Center.

While dating Chip, she heard about Boogie. She met him in 2004, found him likeable, but knew him only superficially. Soon she was dealing with a larger issue: Chip was dying. A melanoma metastasized though much of his body and brain, and by 2008 he was gone.

At Chip's funeral, Boogie delivered one of the eulogies. Several of the old diner guys offered words. Then, in typical fashion, Boogie slipped back to the podium and delivered a second eulogy.

"Forgot to mention a few things the first time up," he said.

As Boogie remembers it, he bumped into Gail several years later and quickly asked her out. He was still recuperating from the cancer, but his toughest days were behind him now.

As Gail remembers it, "It was horrendous, what he went through. The worst of it was over when we started seeing each other. He was still having trouble chewing and swallowing. But his weight was up to about 140, and within a year or so, he was doing much better."

"Gail changed my entire life when I met her," he says. "I've never been happier in my life, except when my kids were born. When I'm with her, she makes me feel special. You first see her, you think she's a stereotyped blonde. But she's smart as hell. You don't get to run a cardiac rehab program just because you're a pretty blonde."

They married in the summer of 2018.

Though she'd learned the classic stories in her years with Chip, she found Boogie different from the legends.

"I was surprised how loving he is," she said. "He tells me five hundred times a day how much he loves me. He's the most caring person imaginable. He's beyond philanthropic. He gives to people, not to have his name on a building, but to make sure they're okay.

"He remembers where he came from. He truly remembers. If he can't give money away, he's not happy. It's always, 'Can we help with this?' And I want to make him happy, because he makes everybody else happy."

They spend part of each year in Baltimore, where they hang out with old friends. Parts of the year, they're running off to visit out-of-town friends or relatives. Part of the year, they're back in Aspen.

They're still active in charities there, and he's still dispensing money to individuals as well as organizations. They still host a big party for the Buddy program every year. In the summer of 2021, more than 300 people came to the ranch and raised huge money for needy children.

Gail is Boogie's best friend above all, his companion as he downshifts toward eight full decades. She is his comfort, his accompanist, the final great love of his life.

Their lives are simpler than before. He likes to sit by one of his big picture windows and stare out at the vastness of his ranch. They stroll around downtown Aspen some afternoons. He's mellowed, and he's reflective. He likes to contemplate the distance he's traveled, from poverty to wealth, from sickness to health, from addiction to recovery, from all that youthful hunger to the realization that his generosity has helped many who needed a helping hand the way he once did.

Along the way, there have been grand days and awful ones. But always, as the big money first arrived, a guiding principle kicked in, and held: Life is more than money.

"All these rich people," he said once, in the first blush of wealth, "and not one of them knew how to enjoy their money. Their lives were wrapped around making more money, instead of enjoying it. And I told myself, 'That's never gonna be me.'"

And it never was.

So let's tell one more Boogie story, because it leaves everyone flying high over America, high over all troubles, and maybe it captures the essence of a man's spirit.

It's the summer of 1979, when Boogie's heading into his late 30s and Merry-Go- Round's bursting its seams and all of his world seems young. So young, in fact, that Boogie's sponsoring a Class A fast-pitch amateur softball team, pretty serious ball, and playing center field. His brother Jackie's there, too, out in right field.

Lenny Miller's one of the team's stars. Lenny's got a serious softball history. He makes his living in insurance, but his passion for sports is so deep that some summers he played 120 games against top-notch regional and national teams.

Now Miller remembers that summer of '79. Two games each week at Druid Hill Park, and one more out in Timonium. Guy named Steve Brickell, who plays first base, spots a story in the American Softball Association newspaper and tells everybody, "Look at this, they're getting ready for tournaments all over the country. There's even one in Las Vegas."

Jackie Weinglass hears this and pipes up, "Yeah, Boogie'll take us."

Everybody laughs, except Boogie. He's thinking about this. A week later, he tells his teammates, "After the game, stick around. I have an announcement."

"This is at Druid Hill Park," Lenny Miller says. It's the soft-ball field next to the Reptile House, just outside the Baltimore zoo. Game's over, and everybody gathers around one of Boogie's limousines, which transport him to all games.

He tells them he looked into the Las Vegas Open Tournament. He says he's taking the whole team, and they should each bring their wife or girlfriend.

Boogie will pay for the whole thing. For everyone. He'll pay for the flights back and forth. He'll pay for everybody to stay in suites at the Hacienda hotel and casino. He'll pay for meals. And he'll give everybody $250 in spending cash.

"After that," he laughs, "you're on your own."

There are 38 people in their traveling party. One night in Vegas, Boogie sits at the blackjack table, with all his pals around to watch, and loses a bundle. Doesn't matter. The grand gesture's the thing, the live-for-the-moment show, the smile.

There are 20 teams in the tournament. They arrive from all over the country. In their opening game, in a scoreless tie, Boogie rips a line drive down the left field line. He's sprinting around the bases, he's thinking inside-the-park homer.

Then reality kicks in.

As he rounds third, he trips and has to hold with a triple. Bloodied his elbow and his chin, feels a little embarrassed. Next guy up strikes out. Now it's up to Lenny Miller to drive him in. He and Boogie confer for a moment.

"I'm so embarrassed," Boogie tells him. "You gotta get me in."

Miller lines the next pitch into left field. Boogie scores, and they've got a one-to-one tie. It's a sweet moment, soured only by an opponent's extra-inning home run and a two-to-one loss.

But, to those like Lenny Miller, the game's only a slice of something far more memorable, which should stay with everyone forever.

They're on the plane from Baltimore to Vegas a few days earlier. Everybody's in their seats except Boogie.

He's thousands of feet in the air, flying high over the whole wide world.

He's boogying down the plane's center aisle, happily singing some great old rock and roll song from back in the pool hall days, back in the endless, giddy diner nights, singing it good and loud.

And he's handing out drinks to all of his friends.

He's handing everybody food.

He's handing everybody cash.

This former dead-end child walking up and down alleys… this swiper of soda bottles for the two-cent deposits…this classroom cut-up written off by every guidance counselor who ever studied a high school transcript…this street fighter whose pants were held up with safety pins…this refugee from pool halls and police cars who heard himself called a dirtball and responded with both fists…

He's flying high over America, he's living the dream, in that rarefied atmosphere few ever know.

Nobody will ever take this life away from him.

He's irrepressible.

He's doing what he loves best.

He's spreading the wealth around, and the fun.

It's beautiful.

It's a smile.

It's Boogie.

About the Author

Veteran author and journalist Michael Olesker spent several decades as a newspaper columnist and television news commentator. On four occasions, he was nominated for a Pulitzer Prize.

He's written more than 5,000 newspaper columns, more than 5,000 TV news commentaries, more than 1,000 radio commentaries, and hundreds of magazine articles over the years.

"Boogie: Life on A Merry-Go-Round" is his seventh book.

Olesker lives in the city of Baltimore with his wife Suzy. They have three children.

In mid-20th century Baltimore, he and Boogie Weinglass attended the same high school, Baltimore City College, and each spent late nights at the Hilltop Diner that was later made famous in Barry Levinson's movie, "Diner."

But, by his own estimate, Olesker was not considered nearly cool enough to be considered a true "Diner guy."

Apprentice House is the country's only campus-based, student-staffed book publishing company. Directed by professors and industry professionals, it is a nonprofit activity of the Communication Department at Loyola University Maryland.

Using state-of-the-art technology and an experiential learning model of education, Apprentice House publishes books in untraditional ways. This dual responsibility as publishers and educators creates an unprecedented collaborative environment among faculty and students, while teaching tomorrow's editors, designers, and marketers.

Outside of class, progress on book projects is carried forth by the AH Book Publishing Club, a co-curricular campus organization supported by Loyola University Maryland's Office of Student Activities.

Eclectic and provocative, Apprentice House titles intend to entertain as well as spark dialogue on a variety of topics. Financial contributions to sustain the press's work are welcomed. Contributions are tax deductible to the fullest extent allowed by the IRS.

To learn more about Apprentice House books or to obtain submission guidelines, please visit www.apprenticehouse.com.

Apprentice House
Communication Department
Loyola University Maryland
4501 N. Charles Street
Baltimore, MD 21210
410-617-5265
info@apprenticehouse.com • www.apprenticehouse.com

CPSIA information can be obtained
at www.ICGtesting.com
Printed in the USA
LVHW081829150322
713510LV00004B/124